STOCKS ARE NOT THE ANSWER

STOCKS ARE NOT THE ANSWER

The Roadmap to a Predictable and Secure Retirement

Tamara Lynn Christians, RFC

Stocks Are Not the Answer

ISBN: 978-1-7325893-0-8

Printed in the United States of America
Year of First Printing: 2019

Cover Design by Ken Wilcox

Disclaimer

While great efforts have been taken to provide accurate and current information regarding the covered material, Tamara Lynn Christians, RFC, is not responsible for any errors or omissions or for the results obtained from the use of this information.

The title, "Stocks Are Not the Answer", is a marketing concept and does not guarantee or imply that you will become wealthy. The act of purchasing any book, course, or financial product holds no such guarantees.

The ideas, suggestions, general principles, and conclusions presented here are subject to local, state, and federal laws, regulations, and revisions of same, and they are intended for informational purposes only. All information in this report is provided "as is" with no guarantee of completeness, accuracy, or timeliness regarding the results obtained from the use of this information and without warranty of any kind, express or implied, including but not limited to warranties of performance, merchantability, and fitness for a particular purpose. Your use of this information is at your own risk.

You assume full responsibility and risk of loss resulting from the use of this information. Tamara Lynn Christians, RFC, is not liable for any direct, special, indirect, incidental, consequential, or punitive damages or any other damages whatsoever whether in an action based upon a statute, contract, tort (including but not limited to negligence), or otherwise relating to the use of this information.

In no event will Tamara Lynn Christians, RFC, or her related partnerships, corporations, partners, and agents be liable to you or anyone else for any decision made or action taken in reliance on the information in this book or for any consequential, special, or similar damages, even if advised of the possibility of such damages.

Tamara Lynn Christians, RFC, is not engaged in rendering legal, accounting, or other professional services. If accounting, financial, legal, or tax advice is required, the services of a competent professional should be sought.

Facts and information in this book are believed to be accurate at the time of publication and may become outdated by marketplace changes or conditions, new or revised laws, or other circumstances. All figures and examples in this report are based on rates and assumptions no later in time than December 2018. Rates and assumptions are not guaranteed and may be subject to change. As in all assumptions and examples, individual results may vary based on a wide range of factors unique to each person's situation. All data provided in this book is to be used for informational purposes only. Any slights against individuals, companies, or organizations are unintentional.

Table of Contents

STOCKS ARE NOT THE ANSWER

The Roadmap to a Predictable and Secure Retirement

Tamara Lynn Christians, RFC

For Jeff –

In our twenty-three years of marriage, you have been at my side as my friend, companion, cheerleader, and the backbone of our family.

Together, we have built a rewarding life and raised two beautiful children.

I am thankful for all that we have together. Your love and support make this possible.

What to Expect!

During the Great Depression, people couldn't trust the banks, so they hid their money under their mattresses!

Stocks Are Not the Answer™ isn't a story about hiding your cash in places where the banks can't lose it. It isn't about buying low-rate CDs or gold bullion either.

There are other ways to accumulate wealth beside risking your money in stocks and mutual funds, and this book is about rethinking risks and accumulating wealth through long-term compound-interest methods that are proven to work. *Stocks Are Not the Answer*™ is designed to show you Predictable Retirement Income Strategies.

And rest assured, the dream of becoming wealthy is not out of reach for the average American. In fact, you are holding the road map in your hands right now.

And guess what? You don't need to be a financial wizard to build wealth. Even if numbers aren't a strength or you're just beginning to manage your finances, my roadmap is simple to read and easy to follow.

But before we dive in, I think it's important to address common questions and concerns I often hear when meeting with my clients.

1. **Is it possible to become wealthy without investing in the stock market?**

   Actually, it depends. My Predictable Retirement Income Strategies aren't for everyone. Some people are addicted to the ups and downs of the market – and believe it or not, they can't understand how their money can safely grow each and every day regardless of the economy, stock market trends, or latest bad news on TV.

   If that's you ... sorry – now's the time to shut the cover of this book and pass it on to someone who wants some security and peace of mind.

2. **Am I too old to start something different?**

   Not unless you are over the age of 80! The concepts presented in this book can be used to grow and safeguard your money for you and your family, starting right now!

3. **Do I have to decrease my lifestyle in order to grow my money?**

   No! In fact, once you discover how *Stocks Are Not the Answer*™ works, you may just end up *increasing* your lifestyle and save money while doing so. There's nothing like living a better life without the heavy dose of guilt or the pressure of a tight budget.

4. **Is this just another high-tech investment advice book?**

   This book is for anyone who is sick and tired of their stomach churning from the Wall Street roller coaster. The principles taught in this book have been around for years.

5. **Is this just another financial scheme? How do I know who to trust?**

   Fortunately for all of us, the solution I share with you in this book has been around for over 100 years. In fact, there's a good chance your parents or even grandparents know about it. You might say that I am bringing some financial wisdom back from the dead!

6. **Do I need to be a financial whiz?**

   Not at all. In fact, I think you'll find the whole process refreshingly simple. You don't need a background in math because you won't need to worry about monitoring the markets or calculating complex equations. Even if you're brand new to managing your finances, once you get going, my Predictable Retirement Income Strategies can run almost like an airplane on autopilot.

Chapter One:

A Reflection of My Family

When you envision your retirement, what do you see? Do you see yourself sitting on a tropical beach with your toes in the sand?

Retirement dreams often vary. Personally, I see myself spending time with my children and, hopefully, grandchildren. You see for me, family really is everything. I enjoy my work, sure, but I work to provide for my children. I want to ensure they have a good life.

It isn't just about providing, however. It's about teaching my children too.

Parents pass down their traits and hope to instill their values in their children. As parents, we want to see our years of child rearing reflected in the adults our children become. Our families help define who we are.

Why am I talking about child rearing in a book about finance?

Because before we talk business, I'd like us to get to know each other, and an easy way to do that is to tell you about my family.

Later on after you have read this book and decide you want a secure, healthy financial retirement, I hope there is a time that I get to know more about you. Without understanding *who* my clients are, what their dreams and goals are, and what is important to them, I simply cannot make recommendations for their future. Despite what you may have been taught, financial planning should be tailored to you – explicitly. You and your financial goals are unique, and your financial plan should be too.

All that being said, I want to start off by telling you about my children – Katherine and Coleman.

Katherine is our oldest child. She just began college at Michigan State University where she is interested in pursuing a degree in Applied Engineering Sciences. She is a smart, loving girl with much to offer the world.

Coleman is a high school sophomore. He is a terrific young man who is kind, has a good sense of humor, and is a supportive friend and teammate. He's talented in many areas, but water polo is his sport of choice.

A Life Measured in School Years

As a mother of two children, many years of my life have been measured not in calendar years but rather in school years.

In our community, there is a tradition of inviting two high school seniors to speak during the eighth-grade graduation ceremony at the end of each school year. The seniors, one male and one female, are chosen by the high school staff.

At the end of this last school year, I received a call from the principal to let me know that Katherine had been chosen.

He told me it was quite an honor to stand in front of 300+ students and their parents. My daughter had been selected to share her words of wisdom and advice.

After Jeff and I sat in the auditorium, glowing with pride as our poised daughter spoke to the crowd, we hurried out to drive north to Mackinac Island. Our son, Coleman, was serving with a group of local Boy Scouts at the Island's Scout Service Camp.

The camp is rich in Boy Scout history, dating all the way back to 1929 when the vice-chairman of Mackinac Island State Park Commission, Roger M. Andrews, invited eight Michigan Eagle Scouts – one of them being future president Gerald R. Ford – to serve as honor guardsmen for the state's governor. They raised and lowered flags, conducted tours for tourists, and fired the sunset gun.[1]

I am equally as proud of my son as I am of my daughter.

The Boy Scouts have been serving as honor guards for the governor's summer residence ever since, and my son was one of them this past year.

Cole is a hard worker and understands service and commitment, and when my husband and I saw him in his uniform, following formation, representing the Boy Scouts, and doing his duty, it was extremely gratifying.

What a wonderful day for two parents!

How We're Raised

I believe our family is a reflection of who we are - we are a reflection of our parents, and our children are a reflection of us.

I'm not trying to toot my own horn, but what I *am* trying to do is tell you more about who I am and what I believe in. My children are a reflection of who I am, and it's a lot easier to boast about them than it is to boast about myself.

It's also easy to boast about my parents, specifically my dad, Wally, and my step-dad, Al.

But before I get to Wally (his influence is most directly related to the content of this book), I want to talk about Al.

My Step-Father, the Astronaut

Al was a NASA-trained astronaut and has been to the moon. My step-dad has been to the moon!

NASA: Astronaut Requirements

To be a NASA astronaut, you have to have a bachelor's degree in engineering, biological science, physical science, computer science, or mathematics, and at least three years of related professional experience (carried out after completion of the degree) or 1,000 hours of pilot-in-command time on jet aircraft(s). You must also have the ability to pass NASA's long-duration astronaut physical and have 20/20 vision in both eyes (glasses are acceptable). Finally, you have to demonstrate skills in communication, teamwork, and leadership.

These are the skills listed on NASA's website, and despite the intensely challenging prerequisites, they received 18,300 applications in 2016.

Do you know how many people they accepted into the program?

They only accepted 60. *Sixty!* That's less than 0.5%[2]!

Once accepted, astronauts must complete a rigorous two-year training program before testing to qualify for flight.

And of course, Al had to do all of that. He had to meet the requirements, pass the interview process, and complete the training program. It required discipline, endurance, mental and physical strength as well as courage and determination. It wasn't easy, but he did it ... and he flew to the moon!

My step-dad, Al, passed those skills down to me. My parents divorced at a young age, but I was lucky that they both married wonderful, positively influential people. Al taught me the value of hard work and honesty – skills that have helped my clients grow their wealth and safeguard their retirement.

My Father, the Self-Made Man

My birth dad is self-made. Everything I learned about finance, I learned from him.

This book is going to be chock-full of financial information. That's why you picked it up and decided to read it, right?

So it really wouldn't be fitting to dive into that information without first introducing you to the man whose footsteps I'm following – my dad, Wally.

(I promise I will get to all those juicy financial details in the upcoming chapters.)

We are a reflection of our families, and our families are a reflection of us. My children are a reflection of my discipline and tenacity, and I am a reflection of Al's honesty and hard work.

These characteristics, in and of themselves, are valuable, but my financial skills and expertise are primarily accredited to my dad, Wally. In fact, throughout this book, I will share his knowledge and experience along with my own.

And why not?

He had a *very* successful career spanning over two decades as a wealth manager and retirement planner and made a highly reputable name for himself in Tampa, Florida. He has worked with nearly 2,000 clients, teaching them how to secure their retirement and gain strong earnings on their savings. He is my father as well as my mentor and has taught me valuable proprietary information that I will share with you throughout this book.

What Do You Believe In?

What do you believe in?

I believe in hard work, discipline, honesty, and integrity. I believe in Predictable Retirement Income Strategies because I believe in secure retirement planning. I want everyone to have peace of mind in retirement, and I am passionate about helping my clients achieve it.

In this book, we will explore the financial challenges facing retirees today and the obstacles you may not even know exist. We're also going to talk about *solutions* – actionable strategies that can give you the security you deserve in retirement.

Many of you are worried about running out of money in retirement.

Let's find out why, and see what I can do to fix that.

Chapter Two:

Afraid of Running Out of Money in Retirement?

I'm not sure exactly when it began, but I have had a fear of cancer for some time now. I can't explain where the root of this fear comes from, but the very idea of cancer terrifies me.

Only recently did my darkest fears come true. In 2013, three women in my family died of cancer – my mother, my step-mother, and my step-sister.

I felt the loss of my mother the most as we were very close. She died at the young age of 70. She was a loving and caring mother and grandmother. She was a strong, independent woman who taught me to not only be strong but to also hold my own and stand up for what I believe in.

Needless to say, our family was devastated. *I* was devastated. These women all died too young, and it left a huge hole in our family.

There isn't a day that goes by that I don't feel the loss.

We all know that we should live each day to the fullest, but do we?

We need to enjoy each hour ... enjoy each day.

And wouldn't that be easier if we got our business affairs handled, simplified our finances, and set ourselves up for a safe retirement so we can enjoy our golden years?

Anything Seemed Possible

There is a cancer infecting America.

It isn't the same type of cancer that took three amazing women from my life. It's a financial planning cancer that, if left undiagnosed and untreated, could leave a lot of us running out of money in retirement.

Back in 1950, the United States was recovering from World War II while facing down a new enemy – China – on the Korean Peninsula. We were an exporting powerhouse – one that fortunately escaped the war with all our production capacity still intact.

Our population was also experiencing a boom. We were growing our wealth and expanding our military capabilities. Even after the ravages of war, we had a tremendous group of workers, 20-to-49-years old, and an explosion of babies on the way.

We were a strong, young nation, and anything seemed possible.

Fast forward 65 years.

The picture today is starkly different. Our demographics – and their impact on programs like Social Security – are undeniable.

We're an aging nation facing some big problems, and many of us are worried about our retirement, and rightfully so. We're afraid we're going to run out of money and be forced to reduce our retirement lifestyles.

Forty-one percent of CPA financial planners report that "running out of money" is the number one concern of their clients entering or near retirement. This figure includes wealthy clients with a high net worth[3].

Even the wealthiest of us are afraid of running out of money. Why?

I believe there are five major reasons why people are afraid of running out of money in retirement.

Reason #1: People Are Living Longer

Many Americans are afraid of running out of money in retirement because, overall, we are all healthier and living longer.

In 1950, the average life expectancy for a man and woman in the U.S. was 65.6 and 71.1, respectively[4]. Today, it's 76.4 and 81.2[5], and in a report released by members of the MacArthur Research Network, by 2050, men will live to be 83-86, and women will live to be 89-94[6].

We can't predict the future, but the data shows that humans are living longer. We're living longer, but we haven't necessarily planned for that in retirement. No wonder people are scared.

Sometimes I sit down with clients and say, "You know you're probably going to live to be close to 100, right?"

More often than not, they just kind of stare at me with disbelief dancing across their faces.

"You've got to be kidding me. My dad died at 78."

"Well, things are different now."

And they are. We are all living longer which means we need to plan for those extra years in retirement.

Have you?

Reason #2: Boom and Bust Cycles

People are also afraid of running out of money in retirement because many of us have retirement accounts that rely solely on the success of the stock market.

Deep down, we know the stock market is not the answer, yet many of us invest in it anyway.

At the time of writing this book, the market is on a nine-year Bull Run, but how long will this upward trajectory last? When will the downturn occur?

There are many different predictions about when it will happen, but almost everyone can agree that it *will* happen. It's only a matter of time.

Throughout our country's economic history, there have been what economists call "Boom and Bust Cycles".

My dad and I work with economist Harry S. Dent. A little later in the book, I dedicate an entire chapter to his economic-based financial strategies because he has used known economic and demographic trends to accurately predict major market (and economic) shifts for the last three decades. He predicted Japan's *two* Lost Decades, the 1990-1992 Recession, the 2008 Credit Crisis, gold's meltdown in 2013, and the Dot.Com Boom and Bust[7].

Dent has used Boom and Bust Cycle analysis to precisely predict past market crashes. But exactly what is a Boom and Bust Cycle?

I'm happy you asked.

> A Boom and Bust Cycle is a "process of economic expansion and contraction that occurs repeatedly[8]".

Well, what does that mean?

When the economy is booming, there is job growth and high market returns. When in the "bust" part of the cycle, the economy shrinks, unemployment goes up, and people lose money in the market.

Boom and Bust Cycles vary in length and severity and are crucial to capitalist governments, but the problem is people are relying on the stock market to fund their retirement accounts!

People are afraid of running out of money in retirement because they're afraid the market will crash.

But why are they investing in the first place?

The stock market is not the answer!

We'll cover more about this later, but with everything we already know about how devastating a market crash can be (do 2000 and 2008 ring a bell?), we *should* be afraid if the majority of our retirement savings is tied to the market.

Reason #3: National Debt

At the time of this book's publication, the U.S. debt is a staggering $21 trillion dollars[9] and counting.

Somehow, *someway*, the government has to start paying it off, and as hard as it might be to relate to a number that big, paying off the debt *will* impact you.

The first thing that will happen is interest rates will start to increase. We're already seeing it a little bit. In September of 2018, rates increased from 2% to 2.25%, up a quarter-percentage point, and central bank officials expect them to increase through 2019[10].

Increasing interest rates also limit the amount of private capital available for investments. All of this slows economic growth and leads to lower wages and an overall lower standard of living.

If the national debt continues to increase, the Congressional Budget Office predicts the average income in 30 years will be $5,000 less than it is today[11]. That means less money for you to spend on the things in life you care about, or even worse, on life's necessities.

It also means less money to put away for retirement.

Does the government have any options? Sure. They can pay off the debt to offset rising interest charges.

How are they going to do that?

The best way I can think of is through taxes.

Most of us will agree that taxes *must* go up. It's mathematical; it's simply a matter of time.

That's scary.

Many of us know we are eventually going to have to start using tax revenue to pay off our government's debt.

Exactly *when* we have to pay it – and how much we'll owe – is still up in the air.

On the one hand, if our debt continues on its current trajectory, interest rates will continue to increase and keep our wages low. On the other hand, to pay off the debt, taxes will most likely have to increase. Either way, Americans' ability to save for retirement will be impacted.

The National Debt might be the reason you run out of money in retirement.

Reason #4: The Birth Rate is Declining

The birth rate in America is declining and has been for more than 40 years.

The chart below shows U.S. population by age in 1950 with generations differentiated by color: Henry Ford (50 and older) gray; Bob Hope (black); the Boomers (red).

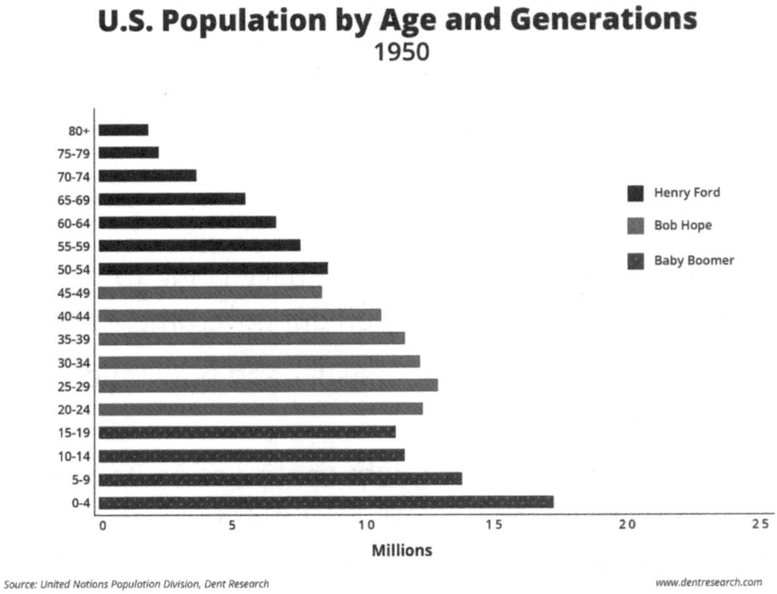

Twenty years later in 1970, the birth wave was over and had begun to recede. The next generation,

"GenX (shown on the next chart), was on the way, but their numbers were much smaller than the boomers.

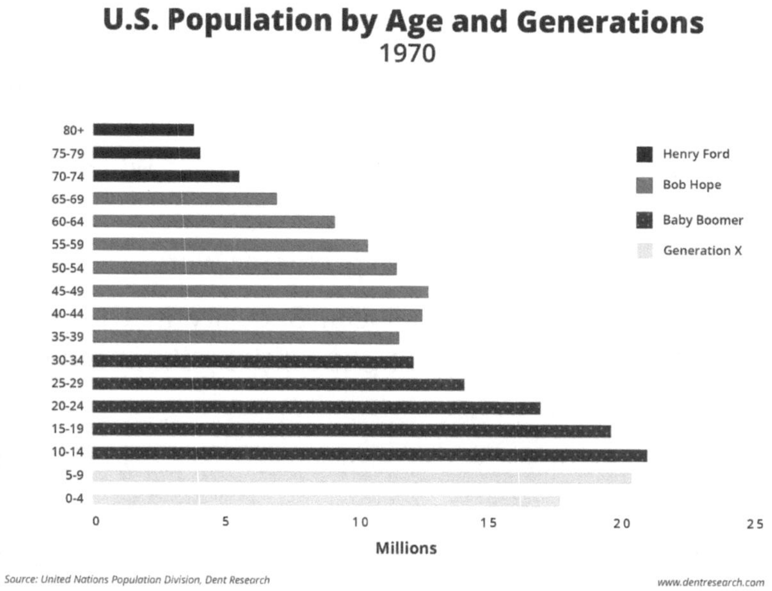

At this point, our demographics and social programs were still balanced. President Roosevelt introduced Social Security in the 1930s, and it relied on workers paying for retirees. With so many workers in the system, the program ran a surplus. Medicare, introduced as part of President Johnson's "Great Society" in the 1960s, tacked on healthcare for the elderly. Again, the program relied on current workers paying for retirees, and as with Social Security, the age structure of the country made the program work correctly ... for a little while.

As the boomers flooded the job market, a lot of extra cash sloshed around in our entitlement programs because they collected a percentage of wages.

However, by the 1980s, our long-term problems with social programs were coming into focus. We had fewer children in the late 1960s and 1970s, so we knew that eventually there would be fewer workers to support a bulging number of retirees.

Longer lifespans made the problems worse.

Congress fiddled with Social Security in the early 1980s, but the reforms just put off the pain and didn't solve the problems.

(There was never an attempt to fix the issues with Medicare.)

Fast forward to 2010, and in the next chart, you can see our society morphing into something else.

We added the millennial generation and even the first years of the next generation, Generation Z. Notice that now the most recent generations are not expanding but shrinking which is much different than the age structure of the nation in previous decades.

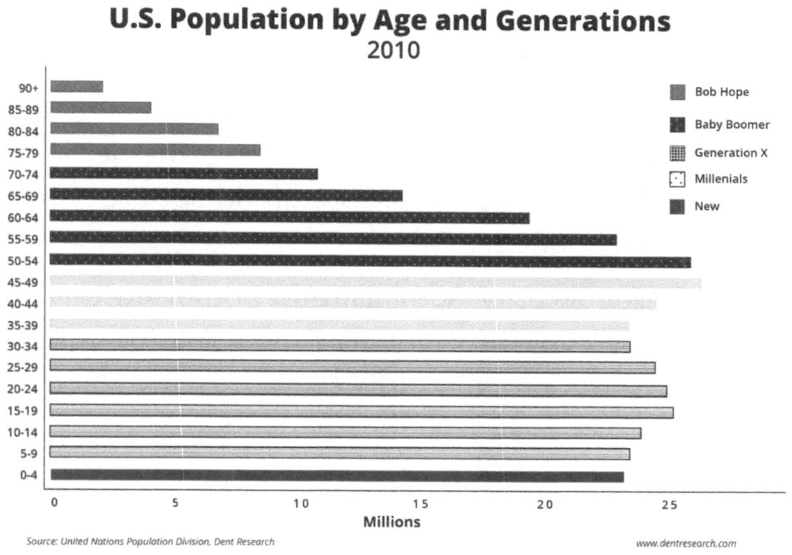

Clearly, we're no longer a nation teeming with strapping young workers who far outnumber the older generation. We don't have younger people who can bear the burden of their elders with a modest payroll tax spread across many workers per retiree.

Instead, we're a nation full of aging adults whose employment statistics reveal more than meets the eye. We look at the younger group with trepidation. With the cost of social programs so high, will the millennials be able to pay the taxes necessary to provide the benefits that boomers have coming to them just as the boomers did for their own parents?

Reason #5: Social Security (or Lack Thereof)

The fifth reason people are worried about running out of money is tied to Social Security. Because of the rapidly increasing national debt (reason #3) and the declining birth rate (reason #4), people are afraid Social Security will become defunded.

The Social Security Administration reported that as of June 2017, one in every six Americans (61 million people) receive Social Security benefits[12], and many of these people rely *solely* on their benefits.

In 2010, Social Security kept 35% of older Americans out of poverty[13], and in 2014, AARP reported that 23% of all Americans relied on Social Security for 90% or *more* of their family income[14].

Many, many Americans rely on Social Security to fund their retirement.

Does it concern you to hear that starting in 2035, the Social Security Administration anticipates being able to fund only 75% of Social Security benefits?

This is the language currently listed on their website:

> *"Currently, the Social Security Board of Trustees projects program cost to rise by 2035 so that taxes will be enough to pay for only 75 percent of scheduled benefits[15]."*

No wonder people are afraid of running out of money in retirement! Anyone receiving benefits in 2035 will see a 25% reduction in their Social Security checks.

A Robust Financial Plan

America is afraid of running out of money in retirement.

Like cancer, the fear is slowly spreading.

And why not? For retirees, the future can be a scary place.

People are living longer, the market is volatile, and our government debt is astronomical. In addition, the birth rate is declining. How can programs like Social Security expect to keep up with the increased costs to support an aging baby boomer population?

I think we all know the answer to that.

But if you're afraid of running out of money in retirement, I'm here to tell you there's hope.

The cancer that shortened the life of my mother, step-mother, and step-sister convinced me to make the most of each day.

I have made good on that promise by planning a secure retirement. How can I make the most of each day if I'm worried about the future?

So what is important for you in *your* retirement? How do you enjoy your days? Would a secure financial plan give you a secure future?

I have said a few times now that stocks are not the answer.

Well, then what is?

I'm going to teach you all about the proprietary Predictable Retirement Income Strategies that gave my dad, Wally, a worry-free lifestyle without the fear of running out of money. Using a straight-forward plan, I'm going to guide you down a financial path where you will see growth in your principle and lock-in your gains – all without losing a penny. You will be able to plan with certainty.

I was (and still am) afraid of cancer, and I recognize that I don't have all the control in that area of my life.

I *do, however,* have control of how I plan for and enjoy my future.

But first, to help you really understand the financial crisis America's retirees are facing, let's talk about the way Americans *used* to retire.

Chapter Three:

The Problem with Your Retirement

One day after the 2008 stock market crash, Wally received a call from a guy who wanted an appointment to meet with him. He explained that he and his wife had $3 million in his IRA before the crash, but it had dropped to $2 million. Dad could sense the pain in his voice, and they set an appointment to discuss solutions.

When Wally arrived to this man's house, he was led into the living area in the rear of the home. He spotted two oversized recliners there, and quickly learned it was where the couple enjoyed watching television and spending the majority of the day. Looking out of the back window, Dad saw a pleasure boat hanging from a hoist. The boat looked like it hadn't been in the water for years.

Dad began the appointment with his standard opening question, "Why am I here?", hoping to learn how they had lost $1 million. He assumed they were scared to lose more money and wanted to keep the remaining $2 million safe!

However, the husband quickly said, "We are only interested in a way to recover the $1 million we lost."

Our Predictable Retirement Income is designed to generate a reasonable return without losing money, and over a ten-year period, many of our clients have earned an average annual interest rate of 5% to 8%.

This couple was not impressed though. They just wanted the $1 million back!

For a brief moment, Wally considered offering a simple and secure solution!

He started to say, "What if you put $1 million in something guaranteed safe with me, and I will get a financial planner to help you invest the other million in a promising investment portfolio."

However, Dad swiftly realized this was not a good idea. They would never be happy with the results.

If the investment portfolio did well, they would be disappointed with our Predictable Retirement Income Strategies and question why they hadn't invested all $2 million.

If they lost more money, they would have wished they had taken our advice to keep the $2 million secure in our safe strategy.

Since it was a no-win situation, Wally had to walk away. He told them we could not work with them.

A year later, the husband called Wally again.

Unsure what prompted the call, Wally asked, "How much money is left out of the $2 million?"

The husband replied, "$750,000!"

Oftentimes, investors just cannot help themselves! They think they know how to manage their own money, and there's nothing you can say to convince them otherwise.

Do You Know How to Manage Your Money?

We know that many Americans are afraid of running out of money in retirement. Like the couple in the recliners, maybe it is because they don't understand how to manage it!

Many people have been convinced by their HR representative to contribute to their employer-provided retirement plan, a 401(k) or 403(b), not understanding that these types of plans are tied to the volatility of the market.

Others have been convinced by some financial planner that they should be diversified and invested in a series of stocks, bonds, and mutual funds to be safe. However, diversification does not guarantee profit or protection against loss in declining markets.

When the market collapsed in 2000 and lost $1.755 trillion in value (more than half of its peak value of $2.948 trillion), investors lost 30% to 50% of their portfolios[16].

Then in 2008, the market collapsed again, and many people were forced to postpone their retirement plans and wait for the market to come back.

Do you think 401(k)s, 403(b)s, and diversified investment portfolios were subjected to all those losses?

You bet they were.

Stocks are not the answer!

Boom and Bust Cycles and market volatility is a problem, sure, but the bigger problem is that most Americans lack the financial information necessary to secure their ideal lifestyle in retirement.

In my opinion, it all started with the change to the way Americans retire – the shift from the pension to the 401(k).

Defined Benefit Plans

From 1875 to the early 1980s, Americans relied on pensions to retire.

Many of us have heard of pensions but don't really know what they are.

Do you?

A pension is a defined benefit plan. It's a fund you and your employer pay into it while you work for the company. The fund – from contributions to withdrawals – is managed by the employer, and it is a set amount, typically a percentage of the employee's salary.

The first corporate pension in the U.S. was introduced by the American Express Company. It applied to employees who had been with the company for 20 years, were at least 60 years old, and had been recommended for retirement by management. A petition for the employee was then presented and voted on by the board of directors and an accompanying committee[17].

According to the Bureau of Labor Statistics, if approved, the employee received half of his salary – up to $500 – to support him in retirement.

Banking companies like American Express were the first corporations to offer pensions. Railroads quickly followed. By the turn of the 20th century, companies like Standard Oil, US Steel, AT&T, and General Electric were also offering pensions[18].

By the 1940s, labor unions joined the growing retirement benefit movement, and by 1960, almost half of the workforce relied on pensions to support their retirement.

Baby Boomers Killed the Pension

For almost 100 years, Americans relied on pensions to retire. Life was worry-free, and retirement - for most - was good.

But as they say, all good things must come to an end.

In the mid-1960s, baby boomers started entering the workforce.

You know why they're called baby boomers, right?

Earlier in this book, we talked about a population boom following WWII. In 1946, the year following the end of the war, 3.4 million babies were born, 25% more than in 1945. In 1947 and 1952, 3.8 and 3.9 million babies were born, respectively. From 1954 to 1964, four million more were born each year, bringing the baby boomer generation total to 76.4 million. At the time, they made up almost 40% of the country's population[19].

When the baby boomers started entering the workforce, the cost of defined benefit plans (pensions) began to become increasingly expensive. Each year, millions and millions of people were getting jobs - jobs that offered pensions.

To top it all off and as we mentioned in the last chapter, people were living longer, meaning corporations not only had to supply *more* people with pensions, they also had to supply them with pensions for *longer*.

Supporting defined benefit plans was becoming impossible, and it wasn't long before corporations started looking for alternative solutions.

Enter Ted Benna, HR Consultant

In 1978, Congress passed the United States Revenue Act. It was enacted by President Jimmy Carter on November 6th of that same year[20].

Around the same time, Ted Benna, an HR consultant, was hired to find a cheaper alternative to the pension.

The bill went relatively unnoticed until January 1, 1980, when it went into effect. Benna, who had read the new code, focused on section 401(k) and created a new benefit plan for his client[21].

As it stood, the law allowed full-time employees to make pre-tax contributions to a company-sponsored retirement account. Benna petitioned the IRS to allow for a company match, and they accepted.

It wasn't long before 401(k)s caught on. By 1996, Americans had amassed over $1 trillion in 401(k) assets with more than 30 million participants[22].

Defined Contribution Plans

No doubt, the 401(k) had replaced the pension.

Think about it.

How many people do you know have a pension?

I can think of a few: teachers, union workers, and government employees.

Most of us have 401(k)s and/or IRAs. Some of us have a pension *and* a 403(b)

On the first day of our new jobs, we're informed of the company's retirement savings plan, a 401(k). We're told our contributions are tax-free and the company will match our contribution, up to a certain percentage.

Since the early 1980s, this is the way Americans has been trained to retire.

But a 401(k), or other qualified account, is a defined *contribution* plan, not a defined *benefit* plan. Defined contribution plans place the responsibility on the employee. You manage your 401(k), not your employer.

You Were Never Taught How to Retire

You are responsible for managing your 401(k), but were you ever taught how to do so?

Does the HR representative ever give you a lesson on the difference between stocks, bonds, and mutual funds?

Rarely, if ever.

Your 401(k) is tied to the market, but you were never taught how to manage it *inside* the market.

So it shouldn't be a surprise that when the market crashes (like it always does), some people lose significant portions of their 401(k) balances.

People are worried about running out of money in retirement. Maybe that's because many are completely uninformed when it comes to managing it.

Say "No" to Investment Accounts

When it comes to planning for retirement, I want all of my clients to be worry-free. I was raised to believe in the value of education and believe that when my clients are armed with the right knowledge, retirement planning is simple and relaxed.

When you work with me, we'll begin the educational process by defining success as the accumulation of wealth throughout your lifetime. This includes retirement when you will be withdrawing money to supplement your Social Security benefits.

And after I get to know you better and learn about what's important to you and what your financial goals are, I will provide you with a written retirement plan.

Like the clients both my dad and I have helped throughout the years, you will never lose any money, you will never pay us any fees, and you will never pay any commissions.

As you might have guessed, I am <u>not</u> going to recommend investment accounts at the end of this book.

Have I been completely clear? <u>Stocks are not the answer</u>.

I wholeheartedly believe in Predictable Retirement Income Strategies, and I will not recommend strategies designed with built-in risk.

What I *will* show you are tools that have created Predictable Retirement Income for my clients.

But more details about that later.

I'll end this chapter by re-stating that I'm <u>not</u> a typical financial planner. Instead, I will teach you how to manage your own money with confidence and without my continuous supervision.

It's easier than most people think!

I continue to state that <u>stocks are not the answer</u>. Even so, I know a lot of you have money invested in Wall Street, so let's explore a stock-market-based retirement plan, otherwise known by many as the *Hold and Hope Strategy*.

Chapter Four:

The Hold and Hope Strategy

A few years ago, a physician with over $3 million of his 403(b) account invested in the stock market came into the office.

His wife was frantic. It was January of 2016, and they had lost over $400,000 in the past two weeks. She was afraid she would not be able to maintain their membership in the local country club.

A written retirement plan was prepared, outlining our recommendation to roll over his 403(b) to a traditional IRA account. The new IRA account featured an immediate 10% cash bonus that would recover $300,000 of the $400,000 he lost. The new $3.3 million IRA account would generate lifetime retirement income, and the wife could stop worrying about her country club dues.

Then came the call.

The physician wanted to wait! The market had started

to show signs of recovery, so he wanted to keep his money invested and see how things turned out.

Another couple called that month, expressing similar fears. They had also lost hundreds of thousands of dollars during the 2008-2009 stock market crash and had never fully recovered. Now they were in their late 60s and losing money again.

A written plan was prepared, outlining how to rebuild their retirement. Then came the call.

That husband wanted to delay as well!

In fact, during that January there were five other couples who went through the same process of realizing their fears, learning about our safe solution, and later deciding to stay invested in the same stock market that had just taken hundreds of thousands of dollars from their retirement plans.

Which begs the question ...

Why doesn't common sense win out?

Wall Street Advertising Is Powerful

Investors encouraged by their financial planners and the media have a hard time relating to Predictable Retirement Income Strategies. The advertising and messaging created by the financial industry is so powerful that most investors will not listen to common sense and continue to lose money no matter what happens!

During January 2016, millions of investors lost massive amounts of money and were once again reminded how quickly stock prices can drop. In February of 2017, it happened again. On February 5, 2017, the market had the single biggest one-day drop in history. It fell 1,175.21 points or 4.6%[23].

And yet, a large number of Americans are still invested in the market. As previously stated, even though investors lost over 50% in 2008 (and didn't recover from those losses until 2015), they continue to believe big money is just around the corner.

Most baby boomers are counting on the stock price or mutual fund gains within their 401k, 403b, and other retirement accounts, and when the stock market reaches all-time highs, it seems as if there's nothing but blue skies ahead.

And stock prices *have* been increasing in spite of a declining economy, an aging population, and massive national debt.

Does that make sense? Isn't that worrisome? Can this continue? Common sense says, "NO!"

But financial planners will always advise clients to stay invested, saying, "The stock market always recovers."

Every financial planner says, "The stock market goes up, the market goes down, but over time, the stock market trends upward."

This *Hold and Hope Strategy* has been followed by

most investors since the mid-1990s. Buy stock and hold on to it – no matter what happens to the market – and hope it comes back.

The *Hold and Hope Strategy* has never created a dependable retirement income! How could it? When you repeatedly make money and then lose it in the market, a predictable retirement income is impossible. How can you predict future income if you lose money?

Many investors recover their lost earnings over time, but the question is, where would these same people be if they never lost those earnings in the first place? If they had used my Predictable Retirement Income Strategy, would they have come out further ahead in the long run?

I'll show you the numbers to prove they would have a little later in the book. (Hint: You're going to like what I show you!)

Stocks are not the answer; there is a better way to save. I can show you how to come out ahead of the stock market using a Predictable Retirement Income Strategy. First, let's look closer at the stock market and its trends.

The Power of the Dow Megaphone

The market ebbs and flows; it has its ups and downs. That's what makes it so unpredictable!

Nothing depicts that more clearly than the following chart:

The Next Dow Bubble Will Burst!
Megaphone Pattern, Dow Jones, Log Scale

Source: United Nations Population Division, Dent Research www.dentresearch.com

What does that look like to you?

The Dow surges then falls, surges then falls, and surges again – like someone speaking through a megaphone.

Economists refer to these surges as **bubbles** and the falls as **crashes**.

Many of us have probably heard the term "bubble", but how many of us really know what it is?

A **bubble** is an investing anomaly that typically occurs when the demand on an asset class is so high that it drives the price far past a rational representation of its true value.

While we're on the subject of definitions, I'll give you another one.

A **crash** happens when the total value of the market drops, and it typically happens when a bubble pops and the majority of investors try to flee the market at the same time.[24]

Bubbles eventually crash. There is no historical evidence showing otherwise. Most of us can still remember the real estate and banking crisis crash of 2008, and many of us can also remember the "Tech Stock Crash" of 2000. Some of us can even remember Black Monday in October of 1987 when the market fell 22.61%[25].

Each of those crashes alone cost many, many investors a lot of money.

5 Key Principles for Detecting Market Bubbles

How can we detect market bubbles?

To spot a stock market or bond market bubble, we must fully understand them. Let's look at the five key principles of the creation of the bubble.

Key Principle #1:

Bubbles begin when stocks or any other financial asset class start growing faster than the linear or fundamental trends, most often well after the bottom of the last major correction or crash.

Key Principle #2:

Bubbles build exponentially for several years – typically five-to-six years in stocks and longer in real estate.

Key Principle #3:

The greater the bubble, the greater the burst. Bubbles vary in intensity which determines both their height and how big they crash. We can calculate the *Bubble Intensity* by taking the "Times Gain" – how much it increased in value expressed as a ratio (instead of a percentage) – and dividing that by the length of time from origin to peak. So for example, if a bubble took five years to triple from bottom to top (a 3-times gain), the Bubble Intensity is 0.60. This calculation permits comparisons to historical bubbles.

Key Principle #4:

Bubbles burst at least twice as fast as they build, more so with stocks than commodities or real estate. The typical stock bubble is about five-to-six years in length with a two-and-a-half- to three-year crash after the peak. (This was the case with the stock bubbles in the late Roaring 1920s in the U.S., the Japan Nikkei bubble in the 1980s, and the 1990s in tech stocks.) The typical real estate bubble is about eight-to-ten years, taking about as long to unwind because they're far less liquid (than stocks).

Key Principle #5:

Most importantly, bubbles tend to go back to where they started at what we call the *Bubble Origin*. Sometimes they don't make it all the way down, and other times they'll drop lower. That's why identifying where the bubble originated is so important. Knowing that along with several other factors gives us a good idea of where the crash will end.

Bubbles and crashes are interrelated; a crash typically happens once a bubble has been burst.

Are we currently in a stock market bubble? Based on the Dow Megaphone, it certainly looks like we are. The real question might be, when will the bubble burst? When will the market crash?

The Big Short

It's almost impossible to detect crashes. If it were easy, there would have been less financial devastation in 2008 when the markets nearly bottomed out.

No one saw that one coming, save a handful of guys.

The movie "The Big Short" debuted in December of 2015 and featured an all-star ensemble cast: Brad Pitt, Christian Bale, Steve Carell, and Ryan Gosling, to name a few. It won the Academy Award for Best Adapted

Screenplay the following year and was nominated for a few others, including Best Picture[26].

The film follows the story of Michael Burry, Front Point Partners, and Jared Vennett and Brownfield Capitol – the three entities that predicted the market collapse in 2007 and made millions hedging against it[27]. Because these guys did what most others couldn't do, a movie was made about them.

If you're invested in the market, how do you detect these market bubbles? How do you protect yourself from losing almost everything?

Like I just mentioned, predicting market crashes is practically impossible.

That's why the *Hold and Hope Strategy* is such a dangerous retirement plan!

Stocks are not the answer. I can't say that enough.

But don't take it from me – the Dow Megaphone says it all. The next crash is coming; it's only a matter of when. So wouldn't it be better to have a plan for a predictable retirement? Wouldn't it be better to invest in something more secure?

After this discussion, many of you might still be saying, "I enjoy playing the market."

I have a special message for you in the next chapter.

Chapter Five:

For Investors Who Like to Play the Market

A dog was hurrying home with a new bone he had just received from the local butcher.

He ran through the town and over a small bridge toward his home in the country. As he crossed over the bridge, he stopped, distracted by his own reflection in the water.

But the dog didn't recognize himself in the water. Instead, he thought it was another dog with a different and much larger bone!

The dog became greedy. Instead of being satisfied with the bone he already had, he dropped it and lunged toward the dog in the river.

In a matter of moments, he crashed into the water, and the bone the butcher gave him fell to the bottom of the river.

As he swam to shore, he couldn't help but feel sorry for himself.

Because of his greed and his desire for more, he ended up with nothing at all.

Do You Love to Chase Gains?

Some of you insist on playing the market no matter the risks.

Like the dog dropping one bone to chase another, you drop money in the market to chase gains - gains that don't even exist yet!

And because you have a positive balance in your brokerage account, you've convinced yourself that you're making good money off your investments.

> It's much easier to remember the wins than the losses, right?

Gambling in Las Vegas is similar. Whenever someone vacations there, he or she is very quick to tell you about the money they won, but do they ever tell you about the money they *lost*?

The casinos in Las Vegas are extremely opulent. In particular, the lobby of the Venetian is tiled with rare Italian marble.

Who is really winning here?

Quite clearly, it's the Las Vegas casinos, not the thousands and thousands of gamblers who travel (and spend money) there.

People Convince Themselves They're Winners

So why do you think people continue to gamble in Las Vegas?

Some are addicted, sure, but many continue to gamble because they have convinced themselves they're winners. They only remember the wins and forget all about the losses.

Your brokerage account is similar. Seeing growth makes you forget all about the losses, so you reinvest your gains, chasing after more and more money. Like the dog, you're quick to drop the bone you currently have and chase after that bigger bone, intent on increasing the balance of your account as quickly as possible.

Playing the market can be addictive for some.

The market isn't addictive for everyone, however. Some people find it's a perfectly acceptable hobby and/or form of entertainment.

If you can afford to separate "play money" from "safe money", go for it! Have fun playing the market!

But if you're chasing gains and relying on the market to supplement your income during retirement, you might end up with a lot less than you need or bargained for, much like that dog.

Predictable Retirement Income Strategies

In the previous two chapters, I showed you just how dangerous and volatile the market has been and will likely be again.

If you love to chase gains and believe very strongly that the stock market is the best tool for your retirement savings, this book isn't for you. You should put it down and save yourself a call because I'm not going to give you "stock tips" or recommend strategies that are directly tied to the market.

I believe in Predictable Retirement Income Strategies – strategies that have worked for Wally, for me, and for our clients.

Throughout the rest of this book, I'm going to share strategies and tips to keep your money safe while seeing growth. I'm also going to show you tools that can provide you with guaranteed income for life.

Can the stock market do that?

Is It Worth It?!

Over the last 20 years, my Predictable Retirement Income Strategies have beat the stock market, and I can prove it!

The Truth About Opportunity Costs

What's the big deal if the market crashes? It always comes back, right?

Losing money is the reason most retirement plans fail!

When you lose money in the market, you also lose the interest that money had the potential to earn had it been invested somewhere else. In the business, we call this an **opportunity cost**.

Let me explain by making a comparison between two couples.

Couple A decided to invest in the stock market; they earned money when the Dow increased and lost money when the Dow declined.

Couple B took our advice and invested in Predictable Retirement Income Strategies.

They each started with $500,000 and began investing in 1997. Both couples were advised to initially withdraw $25,000 – 5% of $500,000 – the first year to supplement their Social Security benefits.

After the first year, the withdrawals increased to adjust for inflation.

Year-End	Withdrawal	Couple A Dow Jones Industrial Average	Couple B Predicable Retirement Income Strategy
1997	25,000	582,540	663,157
1998	25,575	646,581	804,118
1999	25,984	777,111	842,953
2000	26,556	704,171	868,233
2001	27,459	628,665	888,283
2002	28,228	499,804	898,758
2003	28,679	590,320	1,060,452
2004	29,339	578,652	1,100,198
2005	30,131	548,191	1,128,920
2006	31,155	601,262	1,232,687
2007	32,152	605,703	1,290,568
2008	33,053	378,866	1,257,515
2009	34,309	409,402	1,266,018
2010	34,309	416,428	1,274,819
2011	34,858	402,671	1,283,360
2012	35,973	393,320	1,291,045
2013	36,513	451,375	1,298,452
2014	37,093	445,436	1,305,507
2015	37,093	399,237	1,312,808
2016	37,093	410,028	1,319,712
2017	38,528	457,540	1,452,407
2018	39,468	374,634	1,462,392

As you can see, the stock-market-based portfolio plan had $374,634 at the end of 2018.

They may have believed their plan was working!

Our clients, however, never lost money when the market crashed in both 2000 and 2008.

Because of that, even though they withdrew the same amount of money, they ended with $1,462,392 in their account at the end of 2018! Had they been invested in the stock market, their account would have been only $374,634.

The difference between the Dow Jones Industrial Average column and the Predicable Retirement Income Strategy column is the opportunity cost: $1,087,758 at the end of 2018.

Still willing to risk your money?

Why Do Stock Market-Based Retirement Plans Fail?

Many Americans have lost money in the market, yet they are still investing money in it!

Why?

Most people are being bombarded with information from conflicting agendas.

Financial planners (individuals licensed to sell securities) and the media have one goal – to sell you something. As long as you are invested in stocks, bonds, mutual funds, ETFs, and other investments, your financial planner earns an annual fee on money under management in addition to their commissions.

When you liquidate your investments and go to cash in a money market account, this income stops!

The financial industry spends trillions in advertising, and the media prints biased articles to support their advertising sales. That's why your financial advisor will never agree with the strategies I'm emphasizing in this book.

My approach was designed for individuals who don't want to lose any more money. I have a strategy where no one has ever lost any money or paid me any fees or commissions.

Over the last 20 years, the average rate of return has been over 6.50% annually. It is the same strategy many of my clients have used to solidify their retirement savings, and I will teach you how to do the same ... provided you are willing to follow my teachings.

Otherwise, keep looking for gold in the hills!

Chapter Six:

Is Spending Predictable?

What a difference 30 years make ... can you relate?

1970: Long hair
2000: Longing for hair

1970: Acid Rock
2000: Acid Reflux

1970: Moving to California because it's "cool"
2000: Moving to California because it's warm

1970: Our president's struggle with Fidel
2000: Our president's struggle with fidelity

1970: Driver's test
2000: Vision test

1970: Rolling Stones
2000: Kidney Stones

1970: Getting out to a new "hip" joint
2000: Getting a new hip joint[28]

What Are Demographics?

In 1970 when we are young, we may not have had a care in the world, but as we get older, we all worry about spending money, right? Most of us – unless we're independently wealthy – have a budget to maintain.

Some periods of our life are simply more expensive. I have two teenagers that my husband Jeff and I are planning on sending to college.

According to economics and because of our ages and the ages of our children, these are the years of our lives when we're likely to spend more.

Now I'm not an economist, but I work with one who is world-renowned – Harry S. Dent, Jr.

I've spoken of some of his major predictions already, but to be more specific, in 1989 he predicted the end of Japan's economic boom and the beginning of a 12- to 14-year downturn, and around the same time, he predicted a sharp (but short) U.S. recession in the early 90s. He also predicted the boom of the 2000s, expecting the DOW to soar from 7,200 to 14,800 by 2007[29].

I met Harry Dent when I attended my first Irrational Economic Summit Conference with my dad. We are currently among a small group of Lifetime Charter Members and we both hold Master Certifications in the Harry S. Dent Advisers Network.

When it comes to our clients, we use Dent's economic forecasts to provide them with future projections.

Dent's research centers around demographics and spending cycles. His research was (and still is) so compelling that I use his advice for both my own personal wealth-building strategies and those of my clients.

Let me share some of that research with you.

Demographics is the study of birth rates and how many babies are born each year. Demographics directly impact our economy because they directly impact spending.

The table below shows "Strong Uptrends and Downtrends" – periods of time when more babies were being born than less – in the number of births from 1909 to 2008.

Strong Uptrends and Downtrends in Birth

	UPTRENDS	DOWNTRENDS
Bob Hope Generation	1909 - 1914	1917 - 1919
	1920 - 1921	1924 - 1933
Baby Boomers	1937 - 1943	1944 - 1945
	1946 - 1947	1948 - 1950
	1951 - 1957/61	1962 - 1968
	1969 - 1970	1971 - 1973/76
Echo Baby Boomers	1977- 1990	1991 - 1996
	1997 - 2007	2008 -

We've discussed this – the Baby Boomer Generation (1937 to 1976) is massive. The U.S. Census Bureau projects there will be 71.4 million baby boomers in the U.S. by 2029[30].

This matters because in the mid-1980s, the U.S. Commerce Department started collecting data on the consumption of goods and services. The data is used to forecast the sales of most industries.

And they found some patterns.

Predictable Spending from Cradle to Grave

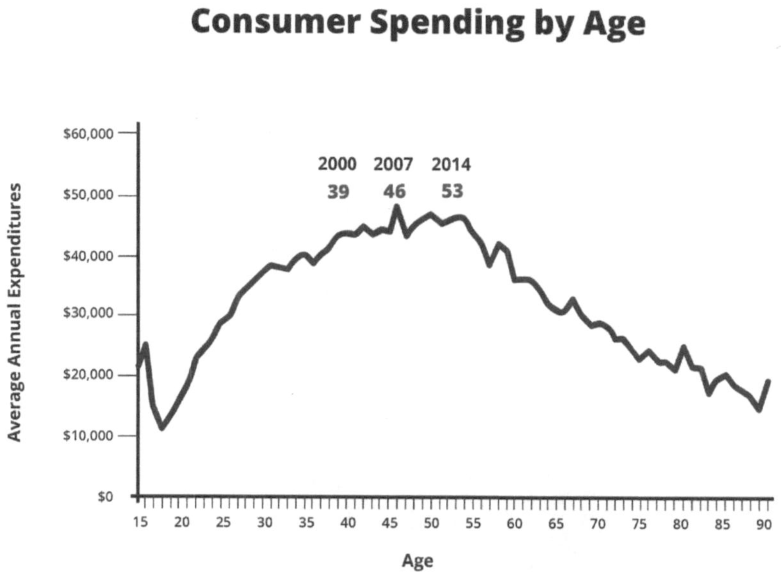

Data Source: U.S. Census Bureau

Using this data, Dent identified the "Peak Spender" population – families whose heads of household are between ages 46-50. These spenders are usually parents of teenagers.

I have two teenage children with one of them just starting college. To say life is expensive right now is an understatement.

What I'm currently experiencing is common for my age group; people with teenagers tend to spend more.

Dent realized there was a predicable adult-spending pattern – from cradle to grave – and recognized the importance of this information.

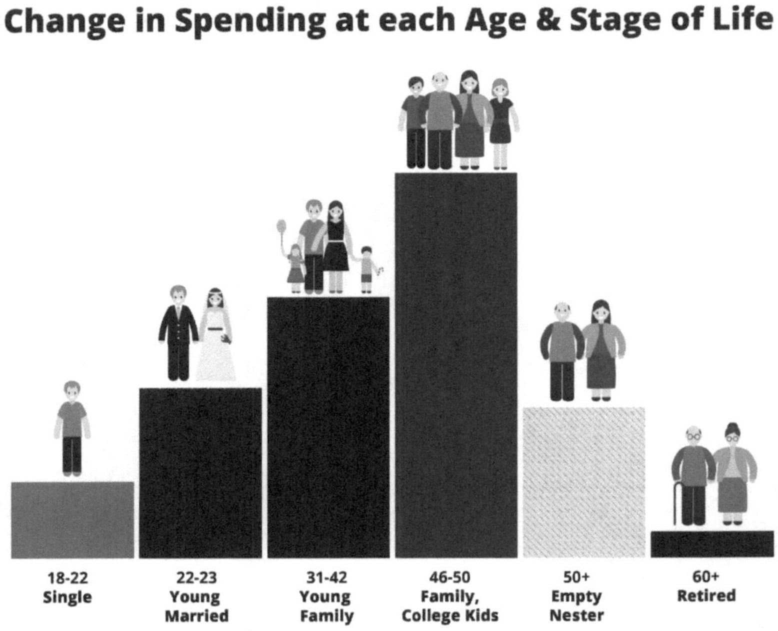

In breaking down each stage of life, can you understand what motivates spending? Can you relate to the predictable spending wave below?

I know that I can. In the last couple of years, our family has spent money on summer camps, computers, high school trips, bigger beds, desks, a prom dress, and an extra car.

Predictable Spending from Cradle to Grave

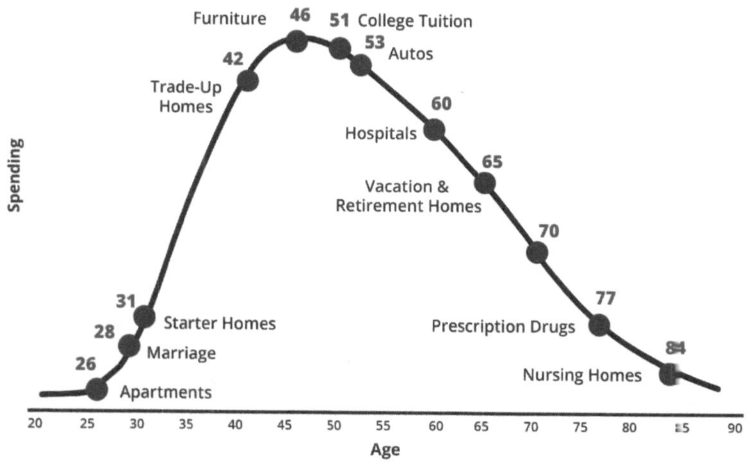

Data Source: U.S. Census Bureau

The Spending Wave

Using all his data on demographics, changes in spending at each stage of life, and predictable spending, Dent put it all together and created the *Spending Wave*.

This is Dent's famous *Spending Wave.* The area is the upward and downward trends of the number of births advanced by 46 years – the middle of the peak-spending period.

For example, if you were born in 1946, you became a peak spender in 1992. If you were born in 1962, you became a peak spender in 2008.

From 1991 through 2008, the Dow Jones Industrial Average grew nearly year after year because the number of peak spenders grew year after year.

When the number of peak spenders started to decline year after year (because of the decline in birth rates), stock prices began to decline because of the trending decline in the sales of goods and services[31].

Why is this wave so important?

The Dow Jones Industrial Average and the S&P 500 Index tend to follow it.

The Health of Our Wealth

There are peak and off-peak spending years for the economy as a whole as well as individual industries within our economy.

You might be thinking, *How does that impact me?*

Economic cycles directly impact the stock market and help create those Boom and Bust Cycles I mentioned earlier in the book[32]. When people are spending money in the economy, business improves, right? A healthy economy typically means a healthy stock market.

The market is affected by the U.S. economy, meaning the health of our economy is directly connected to the health of our wealth. When we understand the economy, we are more likely to have a better understanding of the stock market.

When looking at consumer spending by industries, we can see other trends. For example, let's look at baby boomer spending habits at restaurants, in new car and truck purchases, and for health care.

What's for Dinner?

Did you know that when the first of the boomers reached age 45, McDonald's noticed a drop in sales? Research told them the boomers started seeking healthier diets, so the corporation reacted by offering salads[33].

Restaurant sales are directly affected by the baby boomers – the largest living generation. When the baby boomers first started retiring, restaurant sales dropped.

Out-Aging Their Sports Cars

New car and truck spending is interesting to make note of as well. Sales start to decline once the peak spender reaches retirement.

So what does that mean for our baby boomers who are starting to retire?

They're outgrowing their sports cars and SUVs and trading them in for sedans.

If you think about it, the change makes sense. A sports car is a lot harder to get in and out of than a sedan, and SUVs are unnecessary gas-guzzlers.

In fact, in 2013, 50% of all Mustang buyers were baby boomers, but by 2016, that number dropped to 40%. That same year, Ford Motor Company paused production at their plant for a week when annual sales fell by 9%[34].

New Car and Truck Spending by Age

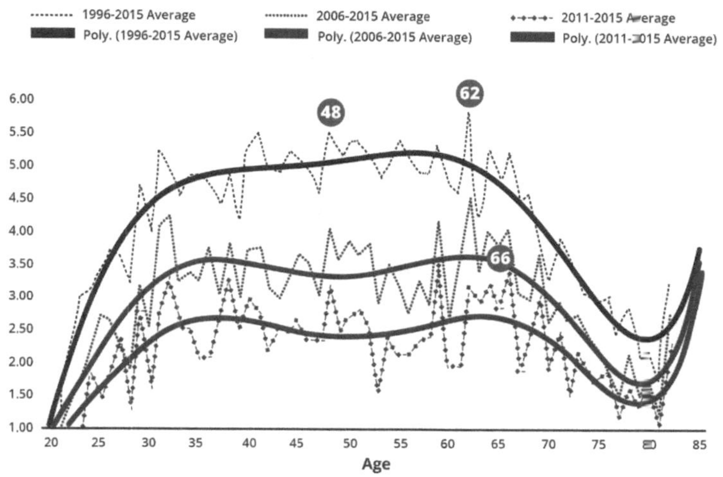

Source: United Nations Population Division, Dent Research *www.dentresearch.com*

A Small Fortune in Health Care

As we get older, it also makes sense that the need for health care increases.

According to a report published late last year, an average 65-year-old couple can expect to pay $275,000 in out-of-pocket health care expenses[35]. That's a lot of money – a lot more than most retirees can spare.

Health Care Spending by Age

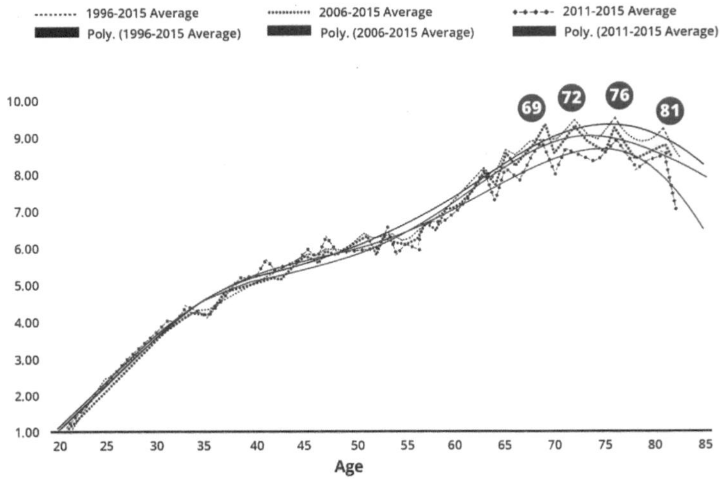

Source: United Nations Population Division, Dent Research *www.dentresearch.com*

Are Peak Spenders Declining?

When the number of peak spenders increased between 1946 and 1960, the national economy was generally improving year after year.

More money was being spent on goods and services which generated a growing economy and rising stock prices.

Make sense?

The number of peak spenders is directly correlated to economic health, and when the number of peak spenders declines, the economy tends to also decline.

In 2008, the number of peak spenders started to decline (and is still declining), and as you are probably aware, stock prices also declined in 2008 and 2009.

That was until the Federal Reserve implemented quantitative easing (money printing) and near-zero interest rate policies. As a result, stock prices increased, but the national debt also increased by trillions of dollars.

What Is Quantitative Easing?

Quantitative Easing (QE) makes is easier for businesses to borrow money; it's a technique used to stimulate the economy by lowering interest rates. Basically, QE is when a central bank buys securities from its member banks to add liquidity to capital markets. In return, the central bank gives those banks a credit for their reserves[36].

Where does the credit come from?

Thin air.

Yes – central banks have the unique ability to spin straw into gold which is why many people simply refer to QE as "money printing".

The U.S. government used this tactic in 2012 to combat a growing financial crisis and bought trillions in mortgage-backed securities and government bonds. From 2008 to 2015, the U.S. government's asset sheet jumped from $900 billion to $4.5 trillion[37].

Fed's Balance Sheet

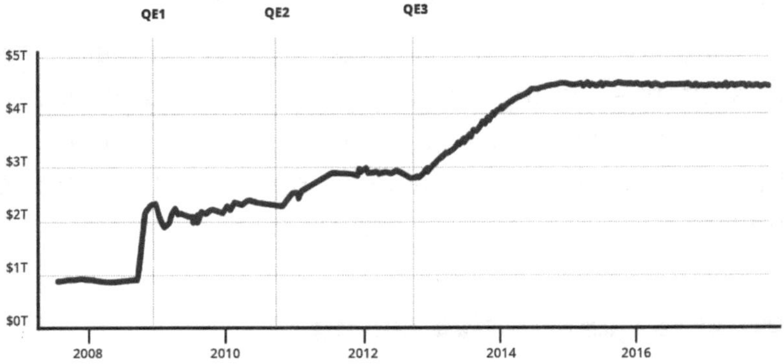

Source: Federal Reserve

So how does this affect your retirement?

Chapter Seven:

A Perfect Economic Storm

Living in Michigan, there are normally a couple of times during the school year when school is cancelled for a SNOW DAY!

Those of you who are parents know that these days are small gifts to our kids, straight from Mother Nature. Nothing makes them more excited than to wake up on a school day, see the yard covered by a blanket of white, and learn that classes have been cancelled. There is usually at least one snow day during each school year.

On one such day a couple of years ago, my son and several of his middle school friends were playing at our house. Toward the end of the day, they all ended up in the hot tub, staying warm with the steam rising around them.

While preparing a snack for the boys, out of the corner of my eye, I saw one of the boys dash by my kitchen window, running through the snow. What were those crazy kids doing?

Even with the windows closed tightly, I could still hear their laughter followed by, "Ready ... set ... GO!"

A few moments later, I watched as two of the boys ran by my window. They were daring each other to run around the house and roll through the snow with just their bathing suits on.

I burst out laughing. I couldn't help it!

I grabbed my phone and took a short video, capturing their screams and laughter.

Looking back, that was one of the worst snowstorms of the season. Businesses were closed, and people lost power. Terrible, right?

But my son made the best out of a bad situation. For him, it was the best day of the year.

Repeating Economic Cycles

In Michigan, we have a typical four-season cycle. We scrape ice off our windshields in the winter, watch flowers bloom in the spring, swim in the lake to kick the heat in the summer, and rake leaves in the fall. We have learned how to acclimate to our weather cycles, and in times of extreme cold or heat, we have learned how to make the best out of our situation.

Is retirement planning any different? Shouldn't we always try to make the best out of any bad situations that may come our way?

Like the four seasons, economic cycles repeat in

regular intervals, and in order to learn how to make the best of these repeating cycles, we can document them for centuries.

So far, we have studied peak spenders and economic cycles that correlate with their decline in numbers.

What you're about to learn is that there are several repeating cycles converging downward at the same time. This is important because it means that hearty economic times are behind us, and we likely won't see another boom for many, many years[38].

In economics, the *Four Fundamentals of Developed Countries* combines:

1. The **39-Year Generational Cycle** - this cycle illustrates when members of a new generation increase, plateau, and then decrease spending as they age.
2. The **34-Year Geopolitical Cycle** - this cycle reflects the global political climate and swings back and forth from favorable to unfavorable every 17-18 years.
3. The **10-Year Boom and Bust Cycle** - this cycle pinpoints crashes, recessions/depressions, and financial crises.
4. A flat **45-Year Innovation Cycle** - this cycle broadly depicts productivity and wage gains. New technology undoubtedly changes how we work and the way we live.

As you can see from the chart below, all four of the cycles are trending downward right now.

The Four Fundamentals
Developed Countries

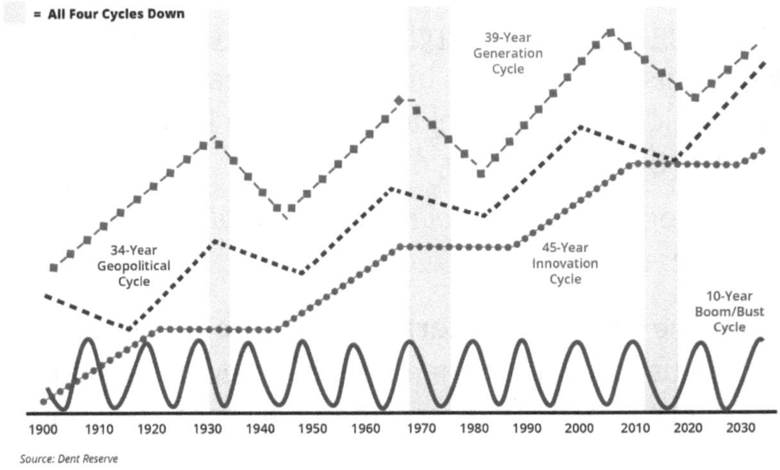

This has only happened four times since the 1800s, and two of those four rare times were phenomena that arguably brought on the Great Depression (1929-1934) and a major recession from 1969-1976, including a stock market collapse and the OPEC oil crisis.

What Else Could Go Wrong?

It gets even worse.

Simultaneously, three completely separate cycles have also been in a declining trend. They are the

250-Year Revolutionary Cycle, 84-Year Populist Movement Cycle, and **28-Year Financial Crisis Cycle**.

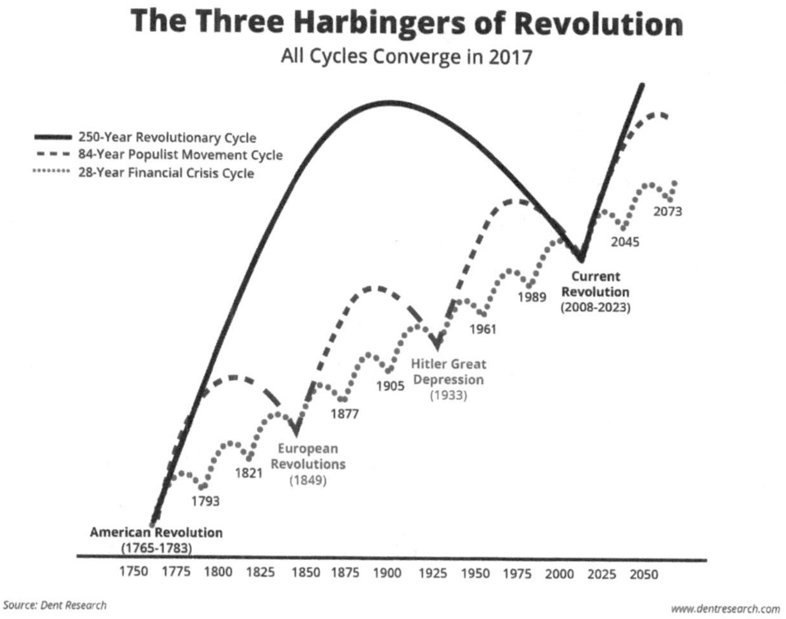

The 250-Year Revolution Cycle is the most turbulent of the three. The last time it paid us a visit was during the American and Industrial Revolutions (1760-1783).

The 84-Year Populist Movement Cycle is also back. We have this cycle to thank for Hitler and Mussolini.

Finally, there's the 28-Year Financial Crisis to deal with too. In 1933, the cycle bottomed out, and we saw the worst of the worldwide Great Depression and the highest unemployment rate in U.S. history. Twenty-eight years later, the next bottom hit, and our economy survived two recessions (1961 and 1962). Finally, it bottomed out again in 1989, and the Savings and Loan Crisis struck in 1990 and 1991[39].

Right now, all three cycles are converging downward at the same time.

What does this all mean?

We already know four cycles converging downward at the same time most likely brought on the Great Depression and the Recession of the 1970s.

What else could go wrong? Plenty.

Dent forecasts that a Political and Social Revolution is on the horizon, and he could be right. We are witnessing early-stage backlash against globalization with much more likely to come. Brexit and President Trump may have started it, but they may not finish it or define the results.

Personally, I believe something even bigger is going to come out of this – a much greater political and social revolution ... a whole new network model for business and our economy.

However, we will have to get back to our cultural and religious roots before globalization and such a network model can advance again.

That might take decades! Can your retirement planning wait that long? Probably not.

A Winter Economic Cycle

The last cycle to discuss is the **80-Year Four-Season Economic Cycle**.

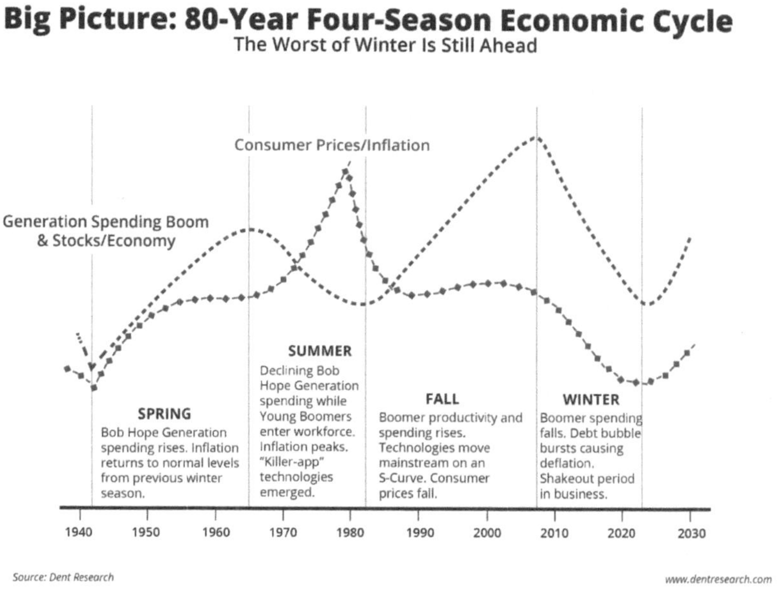

Simply put, this cycle breaks down into:

1. Spring – economic boom, moderately rising inflation
2. Summer – bust in spending, peak inflation
3. Fall – boom in spending, falling inflation
4. Winter – economic bust, deflation[40]

Right now, we are in a Winter Economic Cycle with ten more years to go. And with all those other economic cycles also trending downward, what does that mean for Americans trying to accumulate money for retirement?

That sounds like a really bad winter storm – the kind that shuts schools down for a week.

So how do we make the best out of this situation?

Unprecedented Stock Market Highs?

This all relates to you because it's likely you have money invested in the stock market. You may be invested via a broker or money manager or by contributing to your 401(k) or 403(b). You may have stocks, mutual funds, unit investment trusts (UITs), or exchange-traded funds (ETFs) as part of your IRA.

> Most investment types are allowed to be housed inside an IRA. This includes stocks, bonds, mutual funds, UITs, ETFs, and real estate.

Right now, we're seeing unprecedented stock market highs. In early 2018, 401(k) balances never looked better, right?

This bubble just doesn't want to pop. It finds one way after another to stay alive and keep growing.

But its days may finally be numbered.

Regardless, it's likely going to take something monumental to return markets to reality.

Economic cycle busts are brewing, any one of which – if not a combination of them all – could strike at any moment.

So with the worst of our Winter Economic Season ahead, it's more than possible that our debt will balloon from $21 trillion to $40 trillion by 2024, causing one of those economic cycles to completely bust and bottom out.

What do you think that will do to the stock market?

It's also possible that vanishing job growth will become a problem.

The workforce is barely expanding because of demographic trends. Since the 1970s, our country has seen a gradual decline in birth rates[41].

In an aging society, the workforce becomes smaller as more people retire. There will likely come a point where it's demographically impossible to sustain job growth unless we increase the retirement age.

What do you think <u>that</u> will do to the stock market?

Or maybe the better question is, what do you think all of this will do to your retirement income?

An economic storm determined to wreak havoc on the stock market is on the horizon.

If you aren't prepared and if you don't enlist Predictable Retirement Income Strategies, you might be forced to take a Retirement Snow Day, or worse, a Retirement Snow Decade.

Wouldn't it be better if you could be like my son instead? That snow day was the best day of his year. He wasn't negatively affected by the storm at all!

Wouldn't it be better if you were prepared for that economic winter storm?

Chapter Eight:

The Truth About Global Markets

For the Fourth of July, my family and I like to celebrate at the lake. We BBQ, swim, play games, and watch fireworks. It's always hot, so it's nice to be by the cool water.

One year, my husband Jeff taught our kids to skip rocks.

I watched as Jeff, Katherine, and Cole looked for perfect rocks – ones that were smooth, flat, and easy to throw.

He then taught them how to grip the rock lengthwise between the thumb and pointer finger on their throwing hands.

Finally, he showed them how to throw the rock sideways with a flick of the wrist. The trick was to throw the flat rock like you would a frisbee so it travels parallel with the water.

I specifically remember our children's delight as they watched their first rocks skip across the lake.

Their excitement grew each time a rock landed and then jumped up again. Each ripple in the water was a benchmark of their progress and success.

By the time the fireworks began, I think one of the kids made it up to seven or eight ripples, besting their seasoned rock-skipping father.

It was a fabulous day.

What Happens Abroad ...

That memory got me thinking about the **ripple effect** – a series of consequences caused by a single action.

At the lake, each time the rock skips or touches the top of the lake before flying through the air again, it creates a ripple in the water. The second ripple cannot be created without the first and so on.

The ripple effect impacts everything around us, right? If I'm on a call that runs late, I'll be late to pick up my kids. If I'm late picking up my kids, I'm going to be late for my doctor's appointment, etc.

I believe we can apply this same concept to global economies.

Ripples in water have a multiplying effect. They crash into each other and create other ripples. Global economies work the same way. We are affected by the economies of other countries just as much as they are affected by ours. The effects U.S. peak spenders have on our economy ripple out and impact the economies of the rest of the world. Investors are directly invested in foreign companies or have international mutual funds.

If you think you're safe by investing in American companies, think again. A lot of companies in the United States are impacted by the economies of other countries because they are either buying from them or manufacturing there and shipping goods back to the States.

International markets are critical to investors; they've known that for decades now. What happens abroad has a direct impact back at home.

**Please note that I am NOT suggesting you buy international stocks, so keep that in mind as you read through this chapter. There are ways to invest in international market indexes without the inherent risks of investing directly in the market. Stay tuned for more details in the next chapter.*

Declining Global Peak Spenders

We've spent the last couple of chapters talking about the decline of U.S. peak spenders and the approaching economic storm, but it really doesn't end there.

Global peak spenders in other developed countries are also declining, and because of the ripple effect, we'll likely feel the impact of it here in the U.S.

Let me back up a bit.

Developed countries are very different from **emerging countries**. A developed country like the United States, Germany, or Japan has an industrialized economy and advanced technological infrastructure. An emerging country like Brazil, India, or China is working to rapidly industrialize. Governments of these countries are investing in productive capacity and adopting free market economies[42].

Now back to global peak spenders.

As you can see in the chart below, the number of buyers in developed countries are declining and <u>will continue to decline for the rest of your life</u>.

Global Spending Wave

Developed vs. Emerging Countries (with China Actual to Predicted)

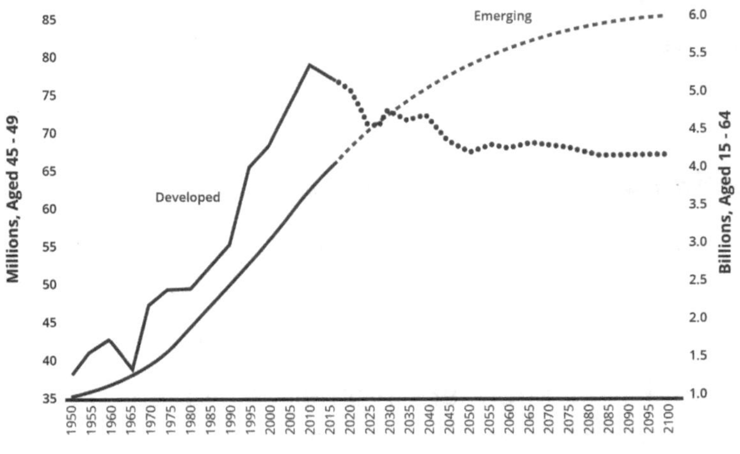

Source: United Nations Population Division *www.dentresearch.com*

We know why peak spenders are declining in the U.S. – baby boomers, the biggest living generation, are starting to retire. Retirees typically spend less, right?

But they're also declining in Japan and parts of Europe and have been for about a decade now. Workforces are aging, and populations are shrinking. Economies are contracting abroad.

To combat the decline in peak spenders and help stimulate the economy, Japan, Germany, and parts of Southern Europe have resorted to **quantitative easing (QE)** and zero interest rates.

And to top it all off, a lot of these countries – particularly Italy, Greece, and Portugal[43] – are drowning in debt.

When you combine QE with bad debt across the region, the financial future of those global economies seems ominous, right?

And if you think banking on China is a safe bet, you're wrong.

China, an emerging country with a massive population, is also seeing a decline in peak spenders. Their population is aging like ours is.

China's working age population is predicted to shrink 5% by 2030 and another 20% by 2050. Many economists think China has reached its peak[44].

Changes In China's Population, 2000 - 2100

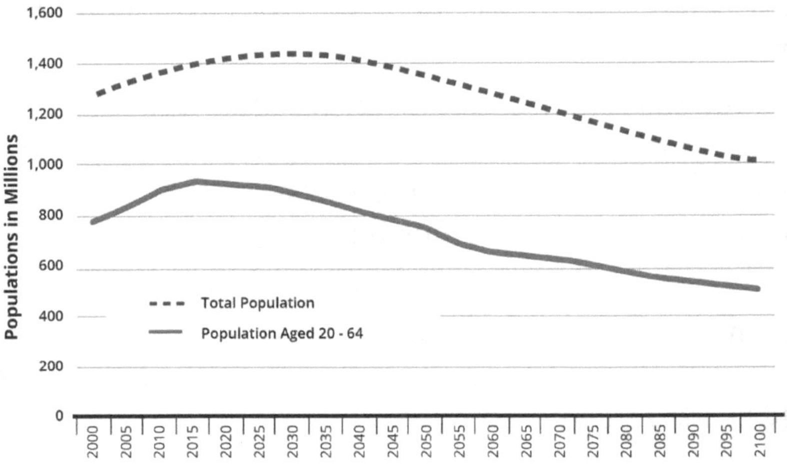

This Chart shows estimates of China's total population and working-age population from the United Nations Population Division. These estimates are based on official Chinese data, which are widely believed to overstate China's true popilation prospects.
Salvatore Babones

As we saw in the previous chapter, a decline in peak spenders typically means a decline in the economy.

Populations are aging, and debts are increasing across the globe.

Yet the markets somehow turn bad news into good news every day.

Does that make sense to you?

Like we talked about in Chapter Five, QE (quantitative easing) is how the government has been keeping things afloat here at home, and as I mentioned, Japan and many European countries are using the technique to stimulate their economies as well.

But how long can that continue? When is "money printing" no longer a solution?

You cannot continue to build an economy without goods and services changing hands. You have to have real people and real demographics of spenders out there who are actually consuming these products. When demand increases, manufacturing and expansion become possible. *That's* how you strengthen an economy.

Emerging Countries Show Hope

There are emerging countries dedicated to investing in industry and production. They are rapidly industrializing and adopting a free market[45].

India is one such example.

India has a population of 1.271 billion – very, *very* close to China's 1.395 billion. It's home to 17.4% of the world's population and is growing at an incredibly fast pace. By 2050, India's population will be larger than China.

We already know China's workforce is shrinking, meaning the possibilities for India are even greater[46].

Economists (including my favorite, Harry S. Dent) predict that it will outgrow every other country for the next 24 years. Late Nobel laureate and economist James Mirrlees stated that India is already twice as productive as China[47].

That makes sense. A bigger population typically means a bigger workforce, right?

At the time of this writing, India's population is 1.3 billion, almost 18% of the world's population. The population continues to grow 1.2% each year and will reach 1.4 billion before peaking. That's bigger than China.

At that rate, India's working-age adults will increase well into the 2050s, possibly even the 2060s. That's a lot of peak spenders for a very long time.

The Pig in the Indian Python Will Drive Investment Gains

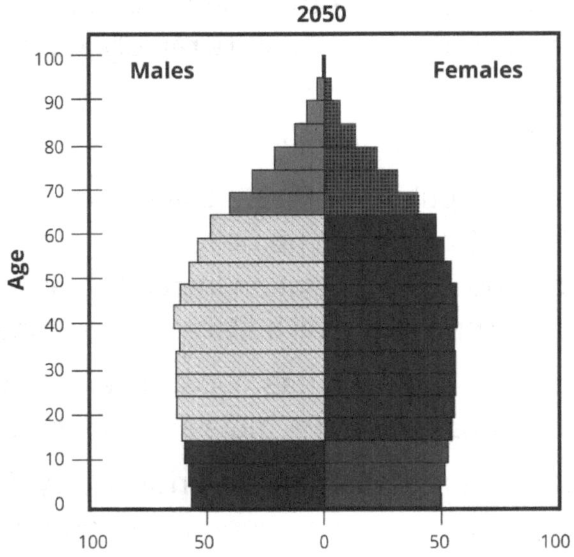

Source: United Nations Department of Economics and Social Affairs, Population Division (2015). World Population Prospects: The 2015 Revision

Peak spenders around the globe are declining, but in India, the workforce and economy are *growing*. And where there is economic growth, there is opportunity. My Predictable Retirement Income Strategies look for growth opportunities such as this around the world.

Other Emerging Markets

Are there other emerging markets we can look to for investing opportunities? Absolutely.

Vietnam is on the brink of being included in the MSCI Emerging Markets Index, a prediction that helped it have the highest performing stock market in Asia in 2017[48].

Brazil is another market to watch. It is the world leader in coffee and sugar production and a major producer of industrial metals as well. Political discourse may impact the ability to invest in Brazil's economy, but they are a country to watch nonetheless[49].

Again, political discord aside, Columbia, Argentina, and Mexico are all on the emerging-markets watchlist as their populations and economies are growing.

But it's also important to note there are major obstacles still ahead for many emerging markets. India needs to build a better highway system and start enforcing trade laws. China has attempted to move people from farms into cities without much success, and many, *many* of these countries have unstable governments.

Is There Hope?

The most important thing to note here is that U.S. markets are only part of the bigger picture. Global markets also impact the stability of your current investments. Like those stones skipping across the lake, changes to any market can have rippling affects seen across the world.

A decline in global peak spenders means a decline in global economies with rippling affects impacting the entire world. Like here at home, the largest Japanese and German populations are moving into retirement, meaning these people will spend less. In China, the workforce is declining too.

And for these countries, it isn't going to get better any time soon. Birth rates in Japan continue to drop; approximately 40% fewer children were born last year than in 1949 when birth rates were at a peak.[50] At best, the economies in these countries will plateau. At worst, they'll contract. This will undoubtedly have rippling financial effects felt across the globe.

So what can we do about it? Is there hope here at home?

The short answer is "yes". According to the U.S. Census Bureau, the population is still expected to grow by 78 million by 2060.

The only problem is the growth will be slow.

We can no longer rely on traditional styles of investing. We need to look for new ideas and new strategies.

Peak spenders in developed countries and China are declining, but in India, Vietnam, and Brazil, young people are entering the workforce in droves. They're earning more, spending more, and giving more back to their countries both in productivity and in taxes. Emerging markets could be the bright spot on an otherwise dark economic future.

But remember I'm not suggesting that you buy international stock. *Stocks Are Not the Answer.* There are ways to invest in international markets *without* investing in the market directly.

The idea here is that the world is full of opportunities, and my Predictable Retirement Income Strategy knows how to find the good ones.

These sure are some uncertain financial and economic times we live in.

Wouldn't it be nice if we could have some stability?

Wouldn't it be nice if there was a way to protect ourselves from the ripples of declining global peak spenders and shrinking international economies?

I'm telling you there is. Turn the page to find out.

Chapter Nine:

Slow and Steady Wins the Race

Throughout this book, I have promised I would tell you a safe way to protect your retirement money while still giving you the opportunity to watch it grow.

Have you heard the phrase, "Slow and steady wins the race"? You might remember this fable ...

Once upon a time, there was an overconfident hare.

All day and all night, he would brag about how fast he was. It was very obnoxious.

One day, he came across a tortoise who he teased and taunted.

"How do you possibly get *anywhere*? You're so *slow,*" he said, rolling his eyes.

"I do quite well for myself actually," the tortoise responded. "I could probably get anywhere faster than you."

"Prove it," the hare sneered. "I challenge you to a race."

He was the fastest animal in the forest. There was no way this slow, boring tortoise could ever beat him.

The tortoise accepted the challenge, and the two decided to race that same day.

Their friend, the fox, volunteered to judge the event. He set the race parameters and established the rules.

"On your mark ... get set ... GO!" he shouted. The race had begun!

The hare was soon out of sight. He wasn't kidding about his speed!

But winning wasn't enough for the hare.

Oh, no.

He wanted to embarrass the tortoise.

So he decided to pull over and take a nap. He would wake up when the tortoise arrived, rub his speed in his opponent's face, and take off again, not stopping until the finish line this time!

He found a cozy spot in the shade, curled up, and fell fast asleep.

Meanwhile, the tortoise continued at his slow-but-consistent pace.

After some time, he passed the hare who was still fast asleep in the grass. He smiled and shook his head as he unwavering continued toward the finish line.

When the tortoise was only a short distance away from the finish line, the hare awoke with a start. He had overslept!

He jolted upright and squinted his eyes toward the

horizon. In the distance, he could make out his opponent about to cross the finish line!

The hare took off at a galloping sprint. He bucked his head and ran the fastest he'd ever run in his entire life.

But it wasn't enough. He crossed the finish line two seconds too late.

The tortoise had won the race[51].

Is Achieving Wealth Any Different?

I think almost everyone has heard a version of that fable at some point during their life.

So what is the moral?

The moral is slow and steady wins the race!

Is achieving wealth any different? My strategy is based on this simple concept, and as you saw earlier, the numbers don't lie. I'll go into that in more detail over the next few pages.

The hare darts from one investment to another, while the tortoise moves slowly through life, continuously making money. The real saver in my version – the tortoise – reaps the benefits of accumulating money in an income-tax-deferred account, never losing any principle through fees or market losses and compounding the interest earned year after year rather than risking his (or her) money and missing the advantages of controlling taxes. (It's the only way to offset inflation!)

Market-based retirement plans can be especially problematic when it's time to withdraw your money. Has your financial planner provided you with any advice on how to use that money to supplement your income during retirement?

A financial planner is an individual who is licensed to sell securities. He (or she) doesn't really want to talk about withdrawals. But if you plan on using that money for retirement, you are going to have to take money out to supplement your Social Security payments at some point in time.

This is where market-based retirement plans can be especially problematic. If you are invested in stocks, bonds, and mutual funds and the market is dropping – which it inevitably will – at the same time you're taking money out, your cumulative value will tank.

This financial phenomenon is called **sequence of returns risk**. If the market crashes during the first few years of withdrawals, you could end up running out of money in retirement.

Throughout this book, I've outlined just how risky stock market-based retirement planning is; I've highlighted the ups and downs of the market and how that correlates to our country's economic cycles as well as the economic cycles abroad. Stocks truly aren't the answer.

That's why I believe in utilizing a secure, unique strategy that combines both financial know-how and economic research. This strategy has also outperformed the stock market.

How?

Because you never lose any money when the market crashes. You never have to worry about sequence of returns risk.

You never have to worry about paying me any commissions or fees either.

And when you don't lose any money, it continues to grow year after year.

Can You Keep an Open Mind?

Before I tell you more about my secure, unique strategy, I'm asking that you keep an open mind.

Can you do that?

Many people are going to hem and haw over what I'm about to share, but the numbers don't lie.

My Predictable Retirement Income Strategies utilize **annuities**.

I know many of you are shaking your heads and crossing your arms.

However, I have found many of my clients simply don't understand annuities. They've heard negative comments about annuities from their son-in-law, their neighbor, and/or their poker buddy and now associate annuities with something negative, but they don't understand what is negative about them. Often a potential client says, "I will never buy an annuity", and when I ask why not, they honestly can't tell me. It's just something they heard from someone else.

It all started years ago when conversations came up about annuities and how terrible they were.

And unfortunately, these unfavorable comments were most often *true* in the past.

It was not uncommon that when you purchased an annuity in the past, you gave the insurance company all your money and kissed it goodbye. You had no control over your money, and if you died prematurely, the insurance company took everything – your heirs got nothing.

Then why do I recommend annuities?

Before you throw this book in the trash, let me explain.

Those complaints were, and may still be, true of *some* annuities, but not all. There are many different types of annuities. Some are good ones, and some I would never recommend to my worst enemy.

For example, I recommend annuities where you can make a healthy return on your principal but won't risk losing money, ever. There are still annuities out there, however, that *do* put your money at risk.

So like I asked earlier, when you hear the word "annuity", please try to keep an open mind. Annuities have grown, adapted, and changed.

The annuities of today aren't the annuities your neighbor/grandparent/buddy bought years ago!

Immediate, Variable, or Fixed?

Like I mentioned, there are many different types of annuities. In my opinion, some are better than others.

The oldest type is a single-premium immediate annuity, and it's very similar to a pension. You give the insurance company a lump sum of money, and they provide you with income for the rest of your life.

There are a couple of problems with these types of annuities.

1. You give up all liquidity of your money. Yes, you will receive consistent income in retirement for as long as you live, but if an emergency comes up, you won't be able to access that money.
2. If you die prematurely, the insurance company keeps your money. It will not be passed down to your heirs.

I don't recommend these types of annuities.

Next up are variable annuities. These are expensive and have the highest fees. They're also risky because they're directly tied to the market. When the market is up, your variable annuity balance might be robust, but when it crashes, your balance crashes with it.

I don't recommend these either. I only recommend fixed annuities. More specifically, Fixed-Indexed Annuities (FIA).

How FIA's Work - In 300 Words or Less

Why do I only recommend fixed annuities?

Because they're safe and will still grow your money.

But a fixed annuity by itself isn't very exciting and doesn't offer as many opportunities to make money. That's why I work with fixed-indexed annuities.

This is a simplified outline of how fixed-indexed annuities work – in 300 words or less.

Annuities are owned and managed by insurance companies. Simply put, they invest your money in bonds. When the market is up, they receive interest payments. About 1% of that is used to pay expenses (and make a profit), and the rest of the money is paid to the annuity owner on each anniversary date.

There are two types of interest rate options: an annually declared rate and an indexed rate usually linked to the S&P 500 Index.

For interest rates linked to a market index, when the market is up and the index increases from anniversary to anniversary, the owner is paid a rate based on the gain.

What happens if the market drops?

Nothing.

If the index declines, the owner typically won't gain anything but won't lose any money either.

That's the true power of my Predictable Retirement Income Strategy – never losing money.

Fixed-Indexed Annuities allow you to take advantage of market gains but protect your money against losses. That's the power of a fixed-indexed annuity strategy.

Imagine that.

The upside of the market without any of the risk!

And that's only *one* benefit of a fixed-indexed annuity.

Another benefit is that you never pay me any fees or commissions.

If you have a brokerage account, you understand how fees can really cut into your account balance, especially during the years when the market is down and your earnings are low. Many times you'll see your account moving backward because of fees. With a fixed-indexed annuity, you don't have to worry about any of that.

Outperforming the Stock Market

What does all this mean? More of your money is working for you.

I want to show you how powerful this approach is by giving you the numbers. I first introduced this example in Chapter Five and now want to explain how my strategy works in more detail.

Let's compare the 2018 year-end account values of two $500,000 accounts opened in 1997.

Year-End	Withdrawal	Dow Jones Industrial Average	Fixed-Indexed Annuity
1997	25,000	582,540	663,157
1998	25,575	646,581	804,118
1999	25,984	777,111	842,953
2000	26,556	704,171	868,238
2001	27,459	628,665	888,283
2002	28,228	499,804	898,758
2003	28,679	590,320	1,060,452
2004	29,339	578,652	1,100,198
2005	30,131	548,191	1,128,920
2006	31,155	601,262	1,232,681
2007	32,152	605,703	1,290,568
2008	33,053	378,866	1,257,515
2009	34,309	409,402	1,266,018
2010	34,309	416,428	1,274,819
2011	34,858	402,671	1,283,360
2012	35,973	393,320	1,291,045
2013	36,513	451,375	1,298,452
2014	37,093	445,436	1,305,507
2015	37,093	399,237	1,312,808
2016	37,093	410,028	1,319,712
2017	38,528	457,540	1,452,407
2018	39,468	374,634	1,462,392

The investor column assumes the stock portfolio gains and losses match the Dow Jones Industrial Average minus a 1% annual fee which is less than most investors pay.

Many companies offer an upfront bonus. The fixed-indexed annuities column reflects a 10% bonus on day one and whatever the account earned from there.

The withdrawals begin at 5% of the initial $500,000 investment and then increase each year to adjust for inflation.

As you can see, at the end of 21 years, the Dow Jones account has $374,634. Many investors may say that's pretty good! But if you look at the fixed-indexed annuity account, at the end of 21 years, it is more than triple the size of the Dow Jones account – $1,462,392.

Why is this?

Because the fixed-indexed annuity account never lost any money. When the Dow Jones Industrial Average account lost money in 2000, 2001, 2002, 2007, 2008, 2009, and 2018, my strategy lost nothing.

This means my Predictable Retirement Income Strategy allows my clients to withdraw more than 5%. My strategy allows my clients to increase their lifestyles in retirement!

Never Lose Any Money

Simply put, my ***Predictable Retirement Income Strategy*** is similar to stock market investing in that it is an account that earns interest based on the gains of a stock market index.

But unlike the stock market, when the index drops, your money stays safe; you don't lose anything.

Like we've already discussed, a fixed-indexed annuity allows you to accumulate money in a safe environment and systematically withdraw money to supplement your retirement.

Because you never lose any money and never pay me any adviser fees or commissions, you maintain complete control of your money at all times, and when you pass, the money in your account passes to your beneficiary.

What's My Secret?

So ... what's my secret?

I have two.

1. It's simple. My strategy is straightforward and easy to follow. You don't have to be a financial guru or have a lot of experience.
2. Your financial planner has probably told you fixed-indexed annuities are bad. Even though he or she is licensed to sell securities and isn't necessarily trained on withdrawing money to supplement retirement income, there may be some truth to their claims. The fixed-indexed annuities of yesterday aren't performing the way they used to.

That's why I now use a new generation of fixed-indexed annuities which are managed by a computer.

And the computer's sole goal?

To find the best way to create a gain in the index given the current daily changes in the markets.

In the past, you would make your annuity investment choice each year and be stuck with that decision until the following year. Meaning, if your annuity index was attached to the S&P 500 and it showed no growth (or worse), you were stuck.

My new strategy is completely different. When you use my Predictable Retirement Income Strategy, the computer tracks the momentum and movement of several different asset classes on a daily basis.

For example, let's say the computer is managing five-to-six different asset classes within an index. If U.S. and international stocks are down, as long as the return will be positive, the computer will adjust the index to take advantage of growing markets – perhaps gold and bonds are going up at that time.

Conservatively, this new strategy projects returns between 6-11% annually, and in the past two years, I've seen 10-10.5% increases.

Another benefit of my Predictable Retirement Income Strategy is a retirement account that requires little to no management!

How Do We Manage Risk?

In the last few chapters, I demonstrated how shaky our economic future could be. There is a glimmer of hope in the U.S. – our population is expected to grow, unlike the populations in Japan and Germany, for example. The economies in emerging markets also look good, and the work forces in countries like India and Vietnam are expanding rapidly.

But as we all know, politics can play a major factor. Venezuela is in an economic free fall. In August of 2018, the value of the bolivar dropped 95%.

How can we leverage the power of international market indices without falling victim to political and economic catastrophes?

That's what makes my Predictable Retirement Income Strategy so powerful. Neither you nor I have to worry about international – or even domestic – political and economic unrest because your money is never directly invested in the market.

My strategy is designed so that you never lose money, no matter how these different asset classes perform.

For example, if your money was tied to the S&P 500 in the past and the market crashed, you were stuck with that choice for a year. You wouldn't lose anything because that's how fixed-indexed annuities work, but you wouldn't gain anything either.

Not only does my strategy ensure you won't lose any money when the markets tanks, it actually allows for adjustments into areas that are growing.

What I Believe In

In today's financial environment, fixed-indexed annuities are the tortoise, and the stock market is the hare.

Yes, the stock market grows faster than my annuity product, but after a crash, it takes a lot longer to catch up!

I believe in secure financial planning. I believe in never losing money which is why I am trained and fully licensed on proprietary wealth-management designs.

We've already talked about the inevitability of another massive market crash. When that happens, will your brokerage account have enough time to catch up and win the retirement race, or will you be forced to either work longer or reduce your lifestyle in retirement?

If you take the tortoise approach and employ my Predictable Retirement Income Strategies, you can not only win that race but also have a secure retirement. My combination of financial knowledge and economic research can help make it possible!

So ... what are you waiting for?

The next market crash is right around the corner, and everyone knows it.

The time to secure your money is now.

If you have not scheduled a complimentary consultation yet, visit www.StocksAreNotTheAnswer.com, or call 800-682-4172 to get started today.

Chapter Ten:

Your Financial Dream

My dad has been a financial consultant for almost 20 years, and in that time, he has worked with thousands of clients. He has led them to a secure retirement they can really enjoy. They can now sleep well at night, knowing their money is protected from market loss.

My dad even told me he believed that helping his clients was a calling at times. Many troubled people would go to him because they didn't know what to do about their financial future. They needed a little simple guidance, and he was able to help.

When I listened to him talk about the clients he worked with, I became inspired. I enjoy working with people and helping them. I love to volunteer in my community and at my kids' schools. I find genuine satisfaction in seeing people happy.

One of my strengths is working with people and helping them solve their problems, so when I heard my dad's stories about the clients he helped, I became inspired to do the same. I decided to take my strengths and *my* desire to help people and use them in a professional capacity.

I like to think I'm following in my dad's footsteps; he's my mentor. I am taking what he has learned over the years and applying it to today's situation. Things have changed a lot in the past 20 years, both domestically and abroad. Navigating today's complicated financial environment is difficult, but it doesn't have to be.

My Predictable Retirement Income Strategy simplifies wealth building and retirement planning. You don't have to be a financial wizard to understand how it works, and you don't need any prior experience. This is a strategy that can work for anyone and everyone.

I have learned that life can change very quickly. When my mom, step-mom, and step-sister passed away within months of each other, our family was devastated, but I learned to make the most of every day because of it.

I think that message is especially important the closer we get to retirement. You've worked hard to get to this point in your life. You've worked hard in your career, and now it's time to make the most of it. It's time to enjoy your loved ones.

What you don't need to do is worry about whether or not you have enough money to get through retirement.

And that's where my Predictable Retirement Income Strategy comes in. I find joy in helping people find solutions. It is incredibly satisfying to assist people as they build wealth and create a secure retirement.

Everyone I work with has a distinct goal and a unique dream. You do too.

Some people have the desire to spend every penny because they want to travel the world. Others very much want to leave an inheritance behind.

But it doesn't matter what your reasons are. If I can help you find the solution to your goals, we'll both be happy.

The sooner you get started, the sooner you can leave that worry behind and watch your secure retirement account grow and grow.

My strategies have worked for so many.

Now it's time they start working for you.

Visit www.StocksAreNotTheAnswer.com or call or call 800-682-4172 to schedule a complimentary appointment.

Are You Looking for a Predictable Retirement Income Strategy?

When it comes to retirement planning and wealth building, *Stocks Are Not the Answer*.

There are other ways to accumulate wealth besides risking your money in stocks, bonds, and mutual funds. I'm talking about rethinking risks and accumulating wealth through long-term compound-interest methods that are proven to work.

You don't need to be a financial wizard to build wealth; my methods can work for just about everyone. Even if numbers aren't one of your strengths or you're just beginning to manage your finances, my Predictable Retirement Income Strategy is simple to understand and easy to maintain.

So what are you waiting for? The next market crash?

Now is the time to take steps to protect your money!

Visit www.StocksAreNotTheAnswer.com or call 800-682-4172 to schedule a complimentary appointment.

Acknowledgements

This book is to serve as inspiration to review your retirement plan and guide you to a predictable retirement solution. I could not have accomplished any of this without the help of others. I want to acknowledge and thank the following people:

My dad, Wally, who has been my mentor and the driving force to help me understand our business and the difference we can make in people's retirement years.

My husband, Jeff, who has believed in me, been a great sounding board, and supported me along the way (he even proofread chapters for me!).

Economist Harry S. Dent, for sharing his many years of study with such passion and inspiration. My financial recommendations have been heavily based on your research and expertise.

My editor, Lisa Caskey, and contributing editors, Brett Kitchen and Ethan Kap of Wealth Education Group, for the months of patience partnering with a new author. Your system for working through this process was extremely manageable, and it's so rewarding to see the final product.

End Notes

1. Suzanne Wilson, "A 75-Year Tradition of Summer Service" *ScoutingMagazine.org* https://scoutingmagazine.org/issues/0505/a-year.html#sbara (accessed November 28, 2018).

2. "Astronaut Requirements" *Nasa.gov* https://www.nasa.gov/audience/forstudents/postsecondary/features/F_Astronaut_Requirements.html (accessed November 28, 2018).

3. Lea Hart, "American's biggest retirement fear: Running out of money" *Journal of Accountancy,* October 6, 2016 https://www.journalofaccountancy.com/news/2016/oct/americans-fear-running-out-of-retirement-money-201615242.html (accessed November 28, 2018).

4. "Life Expectancy in the USA, 1900-1998" *University of California Berkeley* http://www.demog.berkeley.edu/~andrew/1918/figure2.html (accessed November 28, 2018).

5. Larry Copeland, "Life Expectancy in the USA Hits a Record High" *USA Today,* October 8, 2014 https://www.usatoday.com/story/news/nation/2014/10/08/us-life-expectancy-hits-record-high/16874039/ (accessed November 28, 2018).

6. Lauren Cox, "We Will Live Longer in 2050, Study Predicts"

ABC News, December 14, 2009 http://abcnews.go.com/Health/ActiveAging/humans-live-longer-2050-scientists-predict/story?id=9330511 (accessed November 28, 2018).

7. Harry S. Dent, "How Will It All Unfold" *Dent Research* https://pro.dentresearch.com/p/DOW10/EBNBU888/?a=10&o=35629&s=71904&u=1090330&l=651771&r=MC2&vid=YwUoI3&g=0&h=true (accessed November 28, 2018).

8. "Boom and Bust Cycle" *Investopedia.com* https://www.investopedia.com/terms/b/boom-and-bust-cycle.asp (accessed November 28, 2018).

9. "U.S. Debt Clock" *USDebtClock.org* http://www.usdebtclock.org/ (accessed November 28, 2018).

10. Nick Timiraos, "Fed Raises Interest Rates, Signals One More Increase This Year" *The Wall Street Journal,* September 26, 2018 https://www.wsj.com/articles/fed-raises-interest-rates-signals-one-more-increase-this-year-1537984955 (accessed November 28, 2018).

11. Michael Collins, "The National Debt and the Federal Deficit Are Skyrocketing. How It Affects You" *USA Today,* October 16, 2018 https://www.usatoday.com/story/news/politics/2018/10/16/government-spending-how-rising-federal-debt-deficit-impact-americans/1589889002/ (accessed November 28, 2018).

12. "Policy Basics: Top Ten Facts about Social Security" *Center on Budget Policy and Policy Priorities,* August 14, 2018 https://www.cbpp.org/research/social-security/policy-basics-top-ten-facts-about-social-security (accessed November 28, 2018).

13. Selena Caldera, “Social Security: Who’s Counting on It?” *AARP Public Policy Institute* https://www.aarp.org/content/dam/aarp/research/public_policy_institute/econ_sec/2012/Social-Security-Whos-Counting-on-It-fs-252-AARP-ppi-econ-sec.pdf (accessed November 28, 2018).

14. “People Ages 65 and Older Who Rely on Social Security for 90% of Family Income (in 2013) and Average Monthly Benefit (December, 2014) by State” *AARP Public Policy Institute,* November 12, 2015 https://www.aarp.org/ppi/info-2015/people-aged-65-and-older-who-rely-on-social-security-for-90-percent-of-family-income-and-average-monthly-benefit-by-state.html (accessed November 28, 2018).

15. Stephen C. Goss, “The Future Financial Status of the Social Security Program” *Social Security Office of Retirement and Disability Policy,* November 3, 2010 https://www.ssa.gov/policy/docs/ssb/v70n3/v70n3p111.html (accessed November 28, 2018).

16. David Kleinbard, “The $1.7 Trillion Dot.Com Lesson” *CNNMoney,* November 9,2000 http://money.cnn.com/2000/11/09/technology/overview/ (accessed November 28, 2018).

17. Melissa Phipps, “The History of the Pension Plan” *The Balance*, August 21, 2018 https://www.thebalance.com/the-history-of-the-pension-plan-2894374 (accessed November 28, 2018).

18. Melissa Phipps, “The History of the Pension Plan” *The Balance*, August 21, 2018 https://www.thebalance.com/the-history-of-the-pension-plan-2894374 (accessed November 28, 2018).

19. "Baby Boomers" *History.com* https://www.history.com/topics/baby-boomers (accessed November 28, 2018).

20. "Revenue Act of 1978" *Wikipedia* https://en.wikipedia.org/wiki/Revenue_Act_of_1978 (accessed November 28, 2018).

21. "A Brief History of 401K" *Benna 401k* http://401kbenna.com/401k-history.html (accessed November 28, 2018).

22. Tim Stobierski, "401(k) Basics: When It Was Invented and How It Works" *LearnVest,* March 30, 2018 https://www.learnvest.com/knowledge-center/your-401k-when-it-was-invented-and-why (accessed November 28, 2018).

23. Andy Kiersz, "Here Are the Biggest One-Day Point Drops in the Dow's History" *Business Insider,* October 10, 2018 http://www.businessinsider.com/largest-stock-market-drops-in-history-2018-2 (accessed November 28, 2018).

24. Andrew Beattie, "Market Crashes: What are Crashes and Bubbles?" *Investopedia.com* https://www.investopedia.com/features/crashes/crashes1.asp (accessed November 28, 2018).

25. "Black Money (1987)" *Wikipedia* https://en.wikipedia.org/wiki/Black_Monday_(1987) (accessed November 28, 2018).

26. "The Big Short" *IMDB.com* https://www.imdb.com/title/tt1596363/ (accessed November 28, 2018).

27. "The Big Short" *Wikipedia* https://en.wikipedia.org/wiki/The_Big_Short_(film) (accessed November 28, 2018).

28. "Senior Resources" *SeniorResource.com* www.seniorresource.com (accessed November 28, 2018).

29. Harry S. Dent, "How Will It All Unfold" *Dent Research* https://pro.dentresearch.com/p/DOW10/EBNBU888/?a=10&o=35629&s=71904&u=1090330&l=651771&r=MC2&vid=YwUol3&g=0&h=true (accessed November 28, 2018).

30. Kelvin M. Pollard, "Just How Many Baby Boomers Are There?" *PRB.org,* April 16, 2014 https://www.prb.org/just-howmanybabyboomersarethere/ (accessed November 28, 2018).

31. Harry S. Dent, "Capitalizing on the Predictive Power of Demographics" *Dent Research* www.dentresearch.com (accessed November 28, 2018).

32. Aaron Levitt, "Economic Indicators that Affect the U.S. Stock Market" *Investopedia* https://www.investopedia.com/articles/investing/031413/economic-indicatiors-affect-us-stock-market.asp (accessed November 28, 2018).

33. Steven Gray, "McDonald's Menu Upgrade Boosts Meal Prices and Results" *The Wall Street Journal,* February 18, 2006 https://www.wsj.com/articles/SB114022907202077745 (accessed November 28, 2018).

34. David Welch, "Sports Car Sales Fall as Boomers Grow Up" *MarketWatch,* November 7, 2016 https://www.marketwatch.com/story/sports-car-sales-fall-as-boomers-grow-up-2016-11-07 (accessed November 28, 2018).

35. Joel Landau, "Health-Care Dilemma: 10,000 Boomers Retiring each day" *CNBC,* October 3, 2017 https://www.cnbc.com/2017/10/03/health-care-dilemma-10000-boomers-retiring-each-day.html (accessed November 28, 2018).

36. Kimberly Amadeo, "Quantitative Easing Explained" *The Balance,* November 16, 2018 https://www.thebalance.

com/what-is-quantitative-easing-definition-and-explanation-3305881 (accessed November 28, 2018).

37. Elizabeth Schulze, "The Fed Launched QE Nine Years Ago – These Four Charts Show Its Impact" *CNBC,* November 25, 2017 https://www.cnbc.com/2017/11/24/the-fed-launched-qe-nine-years-ago--these-four-charts-show-its-impact.html (accessed November 28, 2018).

38. Harry S. Dent Jr., "Harry Dent's Four Key Macro-Economic Cycles" *Dent Research* 2015 Delray Publishing, Delray Beach, FL.

39. Harry S. Dent, "What the Politicians Don't Know" *Dent Research* https://dentresearch.s3.amazonaws.com/BNB/reports/ZeroHour_pages1-47.pdf (accessed November 28, 2018).

40. Harry Dent, "The 4 Key Cycles That Drive Our Economy Are All Pointing...Down" *Economy & Markets,* January 9, 2014 https://economyandmarkets.com/economy/the-4-key-cycles-that-drive-our-economy-are-all-pointing-down/ (accessed November 28, 2018).

41. Bill Chappell, "U.S. Births Dip To 30-Year Low; Fertility Rate Sinks Further Below Replacement Level" *NPR,* May 17, 2018 https://www.npr.org/sections/thetwo-way/2018/05/17/611898421/u-s-births-falls-to-30-year-low-sending-fertility-rate-to-a-record-low (accessed November 28, 2018).

42. Kimberly Amadeo, "What Are Emerging Markets? Five Defining Characteristics" *The Balance*, October 30, 2018 https://www.thebalance.com/what-are-emerging-markets-3305927 (accessed November 28, 2018).

43. Ashley Kirk, "European Debt Crisis: It's Not Just Greece that's Drowning in Debt" *The Telegraph,* February 8, 2017 https://www.telegraph.co.uk/news/0/european-debt-crisis-not-just-greece-drowning-debt/ (accessed November 28, 2018).

44. Salvatore Babones, "Has China Hit Its Peak? How Demography, Economics & Geography Will Limit China's Growing Power in 2018" *Forbes,* December 31, 2017 https://www.forbes.com/sites/salvatorebabones/2017/12/31/china-max-how-demography-economics-and-sgeography-will-combine-to-limit-chinas-growing-power/#501529fa6433 (accessed November 28, 2018).

45. Kimberly Amadeo, "What Are Emerging Markets? Five Defining Characteristics" *The Balance,* October 30, 2018 https://www.thebalance.com/what-are-emerging-markets-3305927 (accessed November 28, 2018).

46. Harry Dent, "China and India Changing the Global Marketplace" *Economy & Markets,* October 27, 2014 https://economyandmarkets.com/economy/china-and-india-changing-the-global-marketplace/ (accessed November 28, 2018).

47. Max F. Millikan, "National Economic Planning" *National Bureau of Economic Research,* 1967 https://www.nber.org/chapters/c1427.pdf (accessed November 28, 2018).

48. Shuli Ren, "Vietnam Is a Frontier Market for Good Reason" *Bloomberg,* May 23, 2018 https://www.bloomberg.com/view/articles/2018-05-23/vietnam-is-a-frontier-market-for-good-reason (accessed November 28, 2018).

49. Charles Lewis Sizemore, "The 5 Best Emerging Mar-

kets for 2018" *Kiplinger,* January 10, 2018 https://www.kiplinger.com/slideshow/investing/T024-S001-the-5-best-emerging-markets-for-2018/index.html (accessed November 28, 2018).

50. Jonathan Soble, "Japan, Short on Babies, Reaches a Worrisome Milestone" *The New York Times,* June 2, 2017 https://www.nytimes.com/2017/06/02/business/japan-population-births.html (accessed November 28, 2018).

51. "The Hare & the Tortoise" *Aesop's Fables* http://read.gov/aesop/025.html (accessed November 28, 2018).

Made in United States
Troutdale, OR
11/03/2026

56845137R00076